W0016630

新銳舞台系列 New Stage Series

烏合之眾
The Crowd

編劇 · 喻榮軍
Playwright · Yu Rongjun

英文翻譯 · 張菁
English Translation · Gigi Chang

香港藝術節委約
香港藝術節及
上海話劇藝術中心聯合製作
Commissioned by the
Hong Kong Arts Festival
Co-produced by the Hong Kong Arts Festival
and the Shanghai Dramatic Arts Centre

43rd

香港藝術節
Hong Kong
Arts Festival
27.2-29.3.2015

前言

何 嘉 坤

香港藝術節行政總監

在不少表演藝術的歷史中，口述往往是最傳統的記錄、傳承方式，文本、樂譜等是後來才出現的載體。對那個年代的觀眾而言，說書人、歌者、舞者是把作品賦予生命的人。把已寫好的劇本或樂譜搬上舞台，或在創作過程中給予文本特殊的地位，是一項比較近代的現象。今年已經是香港藝術節發行新作劇本的第七個年頭，當我等待那些劇本逐步發展、蛻變、成型的時候，我不禁想起：文本只是一齣創作的起點，只有通過一代代藝術家們的重新演繹，作品才能繼續擁有生命。

你手中的劇本，與作品首演時所看到的應該差距不大。我們不能夠保證這部劇本在最後排演時會否再有改動。倘若此作品會在日後重演，那麼修改的空間可能更大。文字與劇本的編輯與增刪是排演過程中的家常便飯。我們現在發行的這個版本，只能代表本作品無限生命中的其中一個歷史時刻、是作品首演時的一個短暫呈現。然而，在文字、說話皆稍縱即逝的網絡新世代，或許這已經足夠。

我十分感激所有與香港藝術節合作的傑出藝術家，以及藝術節一班充滿熱忱與才華的同事團隊。最重要的是，我要向所有支持我們的觀眾致以最由衷的謝意。

Foreword

Tisa Ho

Executive Director
Hong Kong Arts Festival

Oral tradition predates notation in many kinds of performance. It was the storyteller, singer or dancer who brought a work into existence in front of an audience. Working from script or score, and giving the printed page special authority in the creative process is a relatively new phenomenon. I was forcibly reminded of this while watching and waiting as scripts and texts of 43rd HKAF New Works evolved and developed in this, our 7th year since we began to publish them.

What is in your hands is as close as we could get to what is staged in the Premiere. There are no guarantees that further adjustments have not been made in the final days of rehearsal. And there are likely to be more alterations in the event of a re-run. Texts and scripts are almost always edited in production; what is on the page is a starting point, not the end. What we have published here is therefore no more than a pivotal moment in the work's history. In this age of tweets and blogs and transitory words, perhaps this is enough, especially for words intended for the ephemeral moments of performance.

As always, I am immensely grateful to the wonderful artists who work with us, and inspired by my dedicated and talented colleagues in the HKAF team. Above all, I am deeply appreciative of the brilliant audiences who animate each performance. Thank you all!

編劇的話

文：喻榮軍

「烏合之眾，初雖有歡，後必相吐，雖善不親也。」這是管仲在《管子》有關個體在群體之中變化過程的論述。在人類歷史的進程之中，不管是革命，還是戰爭，不管是民主，還是政治，都是通過群體的變革來推動和實現的，而群體又是由個體所組成，當個體加入到群體之中，個體就不再是原來的個體，他所表現出來的群體特徵往往又和原來的那個個體特徵南轅北轍背道而馳。

《烏合之眾》源於對易卜生劇本《人民公敵》的解讀以及一個真實發生的故事。當權力在沒有束縛的情況下被交到公眾手裏，會產生甚麼樣的後果？為甚麼民眾的訴求會演變成群體的狂熱、盲目甚至盲從，從而失去原本的理智？

一顆自由的心靈是多麼的可貴，但當它被群體的訴求淹沒，沒有約束便會滋生罪惡。一個國家更是這樣，不是毀在獨裁者手裏，就是毀在氾濫的民主手裏。

喻 榮 軍

劇作家。國家一級編劇、上海文廣演藝集團副總裁及上海當代戲劇節總監。

2000年至2015年，已有近50部話劇作品被國內外幾十家劇院上演，並榮獲國內外多項專業獎項。主要話劇作品包括《去年冬天》、《WWW.COM》、《天堂隔壁是瘋人院》、《卡布其諾的鹹味》、《謊言背後》、《香水》、《午夜的哈瓦那》、《人模狗樣》、《活性炭》、《漂移》、《顛天》、《顛命》、《震顫》、《浮生記》、《資本‧論》、《尷尬》、《曖昧》、《老大》及《星期八》等；音樂劇作品包括《你是我的孤獨》及《四兩青春》等；改編作品包括《傾城之戀》、《1977》、《鋼的琴》、《光榮日》、《推拿》及音樂劇《馬路天使》；翻譯改編作品包括《陰道獨白》、《簡愛》、《洛麗塔》、音樂劇《I Love You》，芭蕾舞劇《簡愛》及舞劇《雁丘詞》；戲曲作品包括《紅樓鏡像》及《情歎》。其中16部作品已被翻譯成十多種語言演出和出版，並有20多部作品應邀參加國際戲劇節演出。已出版多部多種語言作品合集。

Playwright's Note

Text: Yu Rongjun

"A motley crew may come together lightly, but with time, repulsion is inevitable – cordial but never close," theorised Guan Zhong in his writing Guanzi about the process of change of an individual among the masses. In the evolution of human history, be it revolution or war, democracy or politics, everything is propelled forward and realised by the reformation of the masses. Yet, the masses are formed by individuals, and when individuals join the masses, they no longer are the individuals that they were. The characteristics of the masses that these individuals manifest often are entirely in opposition to these individuals' original intentions.

The Crowd is based on an interpretation of Ibsen's An Enemy of the People and a true story. When power is given to the public without restraint, what would happen? Why do the people's demands turn into the fervour of the masses, blinding them and causing them to mindlessly follow, to discard their own faculties and logic?

A free heart is hard to find, but when it drowns in the masses' demands, without restraint, it breeds evil. A country is the same: if it's not destroyed by a dictator, it's ruined by unbridled democracy.

Yu Rongjun

Yu is an award-winning playwright, as well as the
director of Shanghai International Contemporary
Theatre Festival and the Vice President of Shanghai
Performing Arts Group.

He is involved with many aspects of the theatrical
community. Since 2000, he has authored more than
50 works for stage and screen. His numerous stage
plays have been performed not only by Shanghai
Dramatic Arts Centre (SDAC) and other theatre
companies in China, but by foreign companies as well,
with productions in Chinese, English, Japanese,
and other languages and dialects. In addition, his
works have been published in Chinese, Japanese,
English and Turkish. Yu has also translated and/or
adapted foreign-language works into Chinese that
have been performed in China and abroad. He has
written screenplays for film and television as well.
As the manager of the Arts Theatre, Drama Salon,
and the D6 Studio of the SDAC, he hosted more than
400 projects for three stages in Shanghai. These
projects included productions from all of China's
major theatre companies as well as more than 200
productions from abroad. He has also facilitated
the world tours of more than 20 SDAC plays. Since
2003 as a dramaturge and producer of the SDAC, he
also has co-produced several productions with foreign
theatre companies.

Yu received Asian Cultural Council Fellowships
in 2004 and 2007 to conduct research on cultural
exchange programmes in the US and was a fellow for
International Residency of the Royal Court Theatre
in 2008.

《烏合之眾》首演於第43屆香港藝術節
2015 年 3 月 27 日香港文化中心劇場

The Crowd premiered at Studio Theatre,
Hong Kong Cultural Centre, 27 March, 2015,
43rd Hong Kong Arts Festival

編劇 · 喻榮軍
Playwright · Yu Rongjun

導演 · 鄧偉傑
Director · Tang Wai-kit

場景及服裝設計 · 王健偉
Scenographer and Costume Designer · Jan Wong

燈光設計 · 黃宇恒
Lighting Designer · Bert Wong

音樂及演場演出 · 黃譜誠
Music and Live Musician · Chester Wong

音響設計 · 任碧琪
Sound Designer · Becky Yam

製作經理 · 蕭健邦
Production Manager · Leo Siu

監製 · 香港藝術節
Producer · Hong Kong Arts Festival

角色及首演演出
Characters and Premiere Cast

楊皓宇 [飾]...... **男人一**

王國慶（二十多歲到六十多歲）、烏鴉、太陽、
兵工廠的工人、買春法官

黃晨 [飾]...... **男人二**

烏鴉、丁建國（兵工廠的書記、二十多歲到七十多歲）、
重慶武鬥中被殺的父親、王國堅（王國慶的哥哥，四十多歲）、
丁立明（丁建國的兒子、上海法官，三十歲左右至四十多歲）、
北京員警、買春法官

蔣可 [飾]...... **男人三**

烏鴉、楝樹、王一清（兵工廠的主任、王國慶的父親）、
上海街角廣場舞者、北京便衣、買春法官

尤美 [飾]...... **女人一**

母親（王國慶的母親）、兵工廠的武裝分子（男）、王國慶的妻子、
丁立明的妻子、雨水、妓女、賓館服務員、清潔工人

劉苡辰 [飾]...... **女人二**

男孩（王國慶，十三歲）、女孩、護士、
丁立明堂妹、妓女、雲層

徐婧靈 [飾]...... **女人三**

烏鴉、野草、兵工廠的工人、重慶武鬥中被殺的兒子、護士、
丁立明的女兒、丁立明的情人、上海街角廣場舞者、餐廳服務員、妓女

註：所有的演員都是敘述者

Yang Haoyu (Cast) ...... Man 1

Wang Guoqing (from his 20s to 60s), crow,
the sun, arsenal worker, lecherous judge

Huang Chen (Cast) ...... Man 2

Crow, Ding Jianguo (secretary of the arsenal,
from his 20s to 70s), a father who is killed during
armed struggles in Chongqing, Wang Guojian (elder
brother of Wang Guoqing, in his 40s), Ding Liming
(son of Ding Jianguo, a judge in Shanghai, from his
30s to 40s), Beijing police, lecherous judge

Jiang Ke (Cast) ...... Man 3

Crow, China-berry, Wang Yiqing (a manager at the
arsenal, father of Wang Guoqing), a dancer in a
square in Shanghai, plain-clothes police in Beijing,
lecherous judge

You Mei (Cast) ...... Woman 1

Mother (mother of Wang Guoqing),
militant from the arsenal (male),
wife of Wang Guoqing, wife of Ding Liming, rain,
prostitute, hotel staff, sanitation worker

Liu Yichen (Cast) ...... Woman 2

Boy (Wang Guoqing, age 13), girl, nurse,
cousin of Ding Liming, prostitute, clouds

Xu Jingling (Cast) ...... Woman 3

Crow, weed, arsenal worker, a son who is killed
during armed struggles in Chongqing, nurse,
daughter of Ding Liming, mistress of Ding Liming,
a dancer in a square in Shanghai,
waitress, prostitute

Note: All actors are narrators

「烏合之眾，初雖有歡，後必相吐，雖善不親也。」

—— 管仲《管子》

人物：男人二 ...... 烏鴉
地點：劇場
時間：現時

【燈光起】

【男人二站在舞臺的中央，黑衣黑褲。他看了看手錶】

男人二：【抬起頭】晚上，七點三十分。劇場。觀眾到場。大幕拉
　　　　開，演出開始。有一隻烏鴉，它口渴了，到處找水喝。
　　　　烏鴉看見一個瓶子，瓶子裡有水。可是瓶子裡水不多，
　　　　瓶口又小，烏鴉喝不著水，怎麼辦呢？我看見旁邊有許
　　　　多小石子，於是就想出辦法來了。我把小石子一個一個
　　　　地放進瓶子裡。瓶子裡的水就漸漸地升高了，喏，我就
　　　　喝著水了。其實，我還可以放別的東西，樹枝啊，蛋殼
　　　　啊，小烏鴉啊。我也可以在地上刨一個坑，讓瓶子斜過
　　　　來，我就夠著水了。我甚至可以在麥田裡找根麥管來吸
　　　　水喝，或者乾脆我就把瓶子推倒，水就流出來了……
　　　　【盯著觀眾】水喝完了，我就飛走了。

【燈光突暗】

人物：男人一 ...... 王國慶，男，六十歲左右
　　　男人三
地點：香港，賓館
時間：2014年

【黑暗中，不安的急促的喘息聲，還夾雜著人的囈語】

【雨聲。雷聲。閃電】

【男人三靜靜地站著】

男人三：2014年。7月。午夜。香港。賓館。窗外。大雨。嘩啦
　　　　嘩啦地下。閃電，從窗戶照進屋子，白色的床單顯得異
　　　　常的陰森。王國慶裹在床單裡，他不停地扭動著，能聽
　　　　到床吱吱呀呀的響聲，都快要散架了。雷聲轟轟隆隆。
　　　　嘩啦嘩啦。吱吱呀呀。轟轟隆隆。嘩啦嘩啦……吱吱呀
　　　　呀……轟轟隆隆……

【雨聲漸停。雷聲消失。閃電消失】

男人三：嘩啦嘩啦……吱吱呀呀……轟轟隆隆……嘩？……吱吱
　　　　呀呀……轟？……吱吱呀呀？吱吱呀呀……吱？

【男人三逐漸地安靜下來】

【男人一在床上扭動著，發出不安的喘息聲，他嚼動著嘴，發出哼哼嘰嘰的含糊不清的囈語】

【突然，男人一發出一聲刺耳的尖叫】

男人一：烏鴉？烏鴉。烏鴉！媽？媽！烏鴉！媽，媽！【尖叫著】媽！

男人三：王國慶掀開床單，從床上一下地爬起來，他喘著氣。

男人一：我站在地板上，喘著氣，牆上的鐘才一點。鏡子裡站著一個男人，看不清楚，他赤條條的，身材並不好，精瘦精瘦的。像只精疲力盡的猴。我得弄點吃的。對，速食麵。路過衛生間。地冰涼的，沒有穿鞋。媽的。

男人三：嘩啦啦……嘩啦啦……

男人一：我打了個冷顫。媽的。

【抽水馬桶的沖水聲】

男人三：洗手間裡沒有燈。

男人一：媽的。

男人三：停頓。

男人一：有兩隻老鼠跑過去了。撞了我的腳。媽的。

男人三：吱嘰吱嘰……吱嘰吱嘰……

男人一：我在背包裡摸到了兩根火腿腸。一把小刀。

男人三：王國慶把火腿腸拿到沙發前，他打開檯燈，仔細地看著。他用小刀小心地切開火腿腸。

【王國慶一邊吃著切下的火腿腸，一邊閉著眼嚼著】

男人三：王國慶在嚼著火腿腸。【咀嚼著】

男人一：我要把他卸成八大塊，然後再一點一點地切成肉塊，一塊一塊的，小小的，放在嘴裡，慢慢地嚼著。【咀嚼著】有些甜，有些勁道，涼涼的，就像是在嚼一塊生牛肉。【咀嚼著】那些組織、那些筋、那些血腥……

男人三：王國慶邊嚼著火腿腸，邊走到窗邊。他拉起窗簾，黑夜下的香港正在暴雨中漂浮著，就像一個高潮過後的女人，肆無忌憚地懶散著身體，在餘歡之中呻吟著。

男人一：我邊嚼著火腿腸，邊看著窗外。玻璃裡，城市的高樓正戳在我昏黃的肉體裡，上下地攪動著。

【閃電。雷聲】

男人三：王國慶看著窗戶玻璃裡映出的自己，那個模糊的、扭曲的、變形的軀體，在閃電之中突然變得清晰而猙獰。雨線就像無數根閃亮的銀針從他的身體裡直直的、斜斜的穿過去。

男人一：我像是消失了，只有黑夜。

男人三：窗外，二十層樓下就是地面，地面是水泥的，濕漉漉的，連成了一片，托起了這座城市。地面上放著許多鐵柵欄，柵欄隔起的地方，坐著黑壓壓的人群，人群向遠處延伸著，看不到邊。它包裹著這座城市，在夜色裡靜默。

男人一：靜默。

男人三：雨，砸在人們的頭上、臉上、身上，雨水順著頭髮、臉
　　　　頰、脖子浸透了全身。他們抬著頭，看著前方。靜默。

男人一：靜默。

男人三：一個、兩個、三個⋯⋯

男人一：一群人，整個廣場，全是人。

男人三：人們浸泡在雨水中，有一種力量順著雨水在流淌。

男人一：蔓延。

男人三：香港濕漉漉的，在雨水中浮浮沉沉。

【砰的一聲，王國慶嚇了一跳】

男人一：一隻烏鴉撞在窗玻璃上，嚇了我一跳。

男人三：烏鴉的身體順著玻璃、跟著雨水一起往下跌落，跌
　　　　落⋯⋯跌落在黑壓壓的人群裡。

男人一：我拉上窗簾。

男人三：王國慶拉上窗簾。

男人一：我嚼著火腿腸，聽著自己咀嚼的聲音。

男人三：王國慶在嚼著火腿腸，他能聽到自己咀嚼的聲音。

　　　　【咀嚼著】

【男人一和男人三都閉著眼，咀嚼著】

【燈光漸暗】

人物：男人一 ...... 烏鴉、兵工廠的工人

　　　男人二 ...... 烏鴉、丁建國（兵工廠的書記，二十三歲）

　　　男人三 ...... 烏鴉、楝樹、王一清（四十多歲，王國慶的父親）

　　　女人三 ...... 烏鴉、野草、兵工廠的工人（男）

　　　女人一 ...... 王國慶的母親，四十多歲

　　　女人二 ...... 王國慶，男孩，十三歲

地點：重慶，兵工廠之間的空地

時間：1967年

【黑暗中，一兩聲烏鴉的叫聲，有些孤獨而淒涼】

【一群烏鴉的叫聲，異常嘈雜】

男人三：樹上有一隻烏鴉。

男人二：呱！

女人三：樹上有兩隻烏鴉！

男人一、男人二：呱。

男人三：樹上有三隻烏鴉！

男人一、男人二、女人三：呱！

女人三：樹上有四隻烏鴉！

男人一、男人二、男人三、女人三：呱！

男人二：樹上有許多烏鴉。

【靜場】

男人三：停頓。

女人三：安靜。

男人二：很聽到陽光的聲音。

男人一：滋滋滋……

男人三：照在身上滾燙滾燙的。

女人三：烏鴉停在樹枝上，他張著嘴，拼命地叫著，卻發不出一個叫聲。

【男人二拼命地張著嘴，無聲地叫著】

男人一：滋滋滋……

男人三：樹葉都捲了起來，無精打采的，蔫了。

女人三：樹枝從工廠的牆頭伸出來，驕傲得很。那是灰白色的水泥磚牆，上面有許多槍眼，子彈打破水泥，露出一塊一塊的紅紅的磚面，就像是人身上佈滿的傷口，呲牙咧嘴的。牆很高，隔著兩個世界。牆上貼了許多標語，標語都是新近糊上去的，在烈日和風還有子彈的摧殘下，早已破舊不堪。牆上有一個大洞，是被剛剛砸開的。一塊磚斷開來，半截伸出洞外，就像條狗舌頭，腥紅腥紅的，赤條條地耷拉在那裡。

男人三：樹長在院子裡，樹幹很粗，上面裂了許多被子彈爆破的口子，慘白慘白的，不停地在嚎叫。口子裡滲出的汁凝固起來，掛在那裡，就像是流出的眼淚。

女人三：樹下全是雜草，許久都沒有人割過，瘋長著，在陽光下恣意地喘著粗氣。

男人三：一棵草，葉、莖、根，生命，充盈著的，清晰。

【女人三是一棵草】

女人三：我的葉上有柔軟細密的纖毛，它能感受空氣的流動，那是風的撫摸。噢！【呻吟著】……我的莖上包裹著薄薄的外衣，它把我的身體裹得緊緊的。噢！【呻吟著】……我的根伸到泥土的下面，那裡濕潤清涼，我可以暢快地吮吸。噢！【呻吟著】……

男人三：陽光！狠毒的陽光。

【男人二拼命地張著嘴，無聲地叫著】

男人一：滋滋滋……

男人三：許多草，許多雜草。

女人三：我不知哪裡是葉，哪裡是莖，哪裡是根。只是一片，一大片，一大片的草，模糊不清。

男人三：街頭的人群，熙熙攘攘，吵吵鬧鬧。重慶、上海、香港。

女人三：他們在說話，他們在爭吵，我聽不清。

男人三：一個人，一個男人，一個穿著軍裝的年輕男人，他站在樹底下……

女人三：一棵樹，葉、枝、根，生機勃勃。

【男人三是一棵樹】

男人三：我大口大口地喝著地底下的水，甘甜的很。【暢快地呻吟著，享受著，突然，驚醒過來】……我呼吸不到空氣裡的水份，我的葉子捲著，疼。【抽搐著】……我的皮膚爆裂開，這該死的陽光……

【男人二拼命地張著嘴，無聲地叫著】

男人一：滋滋滋……

男人三：我把胳膊伸到牆外，風，吹動著我的葉子，捲著的葉子，哪裡都是陽光，該死的陽光……

【男人二拼命地張著嘴，無聲地叫著】

男人一：滋滋滋……

女人三：樹枝上站著許多烏鴉。

男人三：我的胳膊上站著許多烏鴉，我抖了抖胳膊，烏鴉飛了起來。

男人二：呱、呱、呱。

女人三：烏鴉又落回到樹枝上。

男人三：烏鴉又落回到我的胳膊上。

【男人二拼命地張著嘴，無聲地叫著】

男人三：我看到那塊空地，陽光曬在地上，蒸騰著熱氣，那塊地在熱氣中扭曲變形，像是兩個人……

女人三：那就是兩個人，一個中年女人抓著一個男孩的手，他們急急地走著。

【女人一和女人二上場】

女人一：我攬著你的手，急急地走著。

女人二：我快走不動了，媽。

女人一：快點兒。

女人二：媽，我真的走不動了。

女人三：女人與男孩都穿著白色的襯衣，雪白雪白的。這樣別人
　　　　就知道，他們不屬於任何一派。

女人二：媽，我熱，我能把衣服脫掉嗎？

女人一：不行，國慶，再堅持一會兒。他們不打穿白衣服的人。

女人三：女人手裡挎著只竹籃子，裡面放著衣服和一些燒餅，還
　　　　有一瓶水。那是醫院吊藥水後剩下的瓶子，瓶子上面還
　　　　有標籤，瓶子裡面裝著燒開的水，水裡放著幾粒鍋巴。

男人三：水就有了味道。

女人二：媽，我不走了，真的走不動了。

女人一：國慶，你又不聽話了，剛才在家裡怎麼說的。

女人二：下午到了外婆家再歇下來，路上聽媽媽的話。

女人一：這就對了，走。

男人三：全是沙地，非常的開闊，遠遠的，看不到邊。這是兩家
　　　　兵工廠外的空地，平時是共用的。沙地這頭的工廠，製
　　　　造的是坦克，沙地另一頭的工廠，遠遠的，他們製造大
　　　　炮。以前，這裡堆滿了坦克和大炮，坦克挨著大炮，大
　　　　炮挨著坦克。遠遠地看去，分不清是坦克還是大炮。一

片，一大片，模糊不清。三天前，坦克全部被拉回廠裡，就只剩下大炮了。兩天前，大炮也全部被拉回廠裡，就甚麼也不剩了。空空的，一大片的地，除了一兩處因為積水而長出了雜草叢，就甚麼也沒有了。昨天夜裡，砰砰地響起了槍聲，響了一夜，從製造大炮的兵工廠裡打過來，直到天亮才停止。

男人二：陽光很毒，沙子曬得很燙。

男人一：滋滋滋……

女人三：男孩赤著腳走在上面，他燙得跳了起來，他來回來跳著，跳到沙地中央的一塊草地上。

女人二：媽，我不走了，燙。

女人一：那，歇會兒。

女人二：媽，我渴。

【女人把水瓶遞給男孩，男孩拼命地喝著】

女人一：少喝點兒，待會兒還要……

【男孩一口氣把水喝完。男孩把瓶子還給女人】

女人三：女人把瓶子倒過來，幾滴水滴下來，落在草地裡，瞬間就無影無蹤了。

女人一：你看，你全都喝光了，還要走那麼遠的路，就沒水喝了。

女人二：媽，那牆上的字。

女人一：都一樣。

女人二：【辨認著】……槍一響，上戰場……！那有棵樹，媽！

女人一：楝樹，苦得很。

女人二：媽，我不想去鄉下。

女人一：聽話。

女人二：哥哥為啥不去。

女人一：他上學。

女人二：他沒上學。他去打架了。他和爸爸去打架了。

女人一：不是打架。

女人二：是打架，我看到的，他們打人了，爸爸打，哥哥也打。

　　　　爸爸打哥哥的人，哥哥打爸爸的人，他們不是一起的。

女人一：胡說……【稍停】所以，我們去鄉下。

女人二：我不想去鄉下。

女人一：聽話。

女人二：那有棵樹，媽。

女人三：女人看著那棵樹，沒有說話。

男人三：陽光毒的很。

男人一：滋滋滋……

女人三：樹葉都捲了。

男人三：我的胳膊很疼。

女人三：他站在樹下，一個年輕的穿著白襯衫的男人。

男人三：那個年輕的穿著白襯衫的男人站在我的下面，靠著我，手裡拿著把步槍，一把簇新的步槍。

【男人二手裡拿著步槍，他瞄準著，把玩著】

男人一：建國，這槍不錯。

男人三：這批是今天早晨剛到的。我們從八五七廠換來的。

男人一：換？

男人三：一架炮，一百把全自動步槍。我們換了六十多門炮。他
　　　　們划算，他們也在打？跟我們一邊。他們有四千多人，
　　　　我們有六千多人，加在一起，快一萬了。

男人一：一萬人？

男人三：他們也不少。

女人三：每人一把，子彈多的是，隨便打。

男人三：他媽的，敢打我們，不教訓教訓他們，還不知道老子們
　　　　的厲害。

男人一：沒事吧。

男人三：有啥事，打槍誰不會？當年我……他媽的，打了我們一夜。

女人三：司令部說了，小青年愛玩槍，打打也好，練習練習。沒事。

男人三：革命不是請客吃飯，革命就是一個階級推翻另一個階級
　　　　的暴力行動。

男人二：這是一場人民戰爭，我們一定要打贏。

男人三：建國說的對，這是一場人民戰爭。

女人三：丁建國走到牆角下，我搬過去一把舊椅子。

男人二：我站在上面，可以夠著那只牆洞。

男人一：危險，當心他們進攻。

男人三：中午，都睡著呢。

女人三：看到甚麼了？

男人二：啥也沒有？不，有人！

男人一：【緊張地】甚麼？建國，你下來吧，危險。

女人三：你看到甚麼？

男人二：一個女人，一個孩子。

女人三：女人？孩子？

男人三：女人站著，孩子坐著。

女人三：他們在那裡幹甚麼？奇怪。

女人二：媽，牆那邊是甚麼？

女人一：是你爸爸的工廠。

女人二：爸爸在打架。

女人一：走吧。

女人二：媽，我再歇會兒，沙子太燙了，我腳痛。

女人一：就你懶，來，媽背你。

女人三：女人彎下腰，她準備背那個男孩。

男人一：天空藍得嚇人，一絲雲也沒有。

女人三：女人把瓶子放到籃子裡。

男人一：風，有一絲，吹過女人的頭髮，她的頭髮飄起來。

女人三：我葉子上的纖毛動了起來。

男人三：我的葉子動了動，很費力，很痛。

男人一：很多人走過來。

女人三：外面的空地上竟然有人。

男人一：誰？

男人三：管他是誰？找死啊。

男人一：一個上午，他們都沒有動靜，估計要準備進攻了。

男人三：我們得準備起來。

女人三：所有班都停了，人人都武裝起來。

男人一：有幾個逃跑的。

男人三：孬種，慫。

男人二：這槍好使吧。

男人三：你試試。

男人二：試？

男人三：不試，怎麼知道？

男人一：你當過兵。

男人三：以前在朝鮮打過，不殺人不知道這槍有多好。瞄準、扣動扳機、射擊、就完事了。

男人一：就這麼簡單。

女人三：那你得給全廠的人做一下培訓，我們都沒打過槍，還不知道怎麼扣板機呢。

男人二：就這麼簡單？

女人一：甚麼東西擊中我的胸口，我聽見輕微的聲音。是甚麼？鑽進了我的身體，怎麼了？國慶，我們走吧。這地方不能待。是甚麼響？槍響？國慶，快跑⋯⋯

【一聲巨大的槍聲。女人倒地，男孩驚呆】

男人二：準。

男人三：好。

男人一：你打了？

女人三：怎麼樣？

男人二：沒啥。

男人一：你真的打了？建國。

男人三：他從椅子上跳了下來。

男人二：我從椅子上跳下來。

女人三：你打了，建國。讓我看看。

男人二：沒啥看的。

男人一：他把椅子推倒。

男人二：我把椅子推倒。

女人三：椅子砸在我的身上，我的葉子折了，我的莖斷了，痛。

男人三：槍聲震得烏鴉都飛了起來。

男人二：呱、呱、呱！

男人三：槍聲讓我渾身一震。烏鴉從我的身上飛走了。我的葉子落了下來，飄飄搖搖，落在沙地上，真燙。痛。

女人二：【大哭】媽！媽！媽！

男人一：女人倒在地上，血從她的胸口流出來。

女人二：媽，你怎麼了，怎麼了？媽，你流血了。我堵不住，
　　　　媽！媽！

女人三：1967年，7月的一天，中午，重慶，兩座兵工廠之間的
　　　　空地。

男人一：天，很藍。

男人二：沒風。

女人三：陽光很毒。

男人三：烏鴉在空中盤旋。

男人二：我喝了口水，手不停地發抖。媽的，真準。

男人一：我好像聽到有人哭了。

男人二：沒有。

男人一：【傾聽著】是沒有。

女人三：是烏鴉叫。

男人三：是烏鴉叫。

男人一：真安靜。

【男孩坐在地上，看著女人，哭嚷著】

女人二：媽，你怎麼了？媽！你醒醒，我怕，我怕。

男人一：女人的臉，慘白。

男人二：血從她的胸口流出來，汩汩的流出來，流在了草地上。

女人三：草，很綠。我很羨慕，我甚麼時候也能這樣。在中午的
　　　　時候有水把我滋養，哪怕是血水。

男人三：我的那片掉落的葉子在地上捲曲著，枯萎了，就像死人
　　　　的臉，沒有了生氣。

男人一：女人的臉，毫無生氣。

男人二：男孩推著女人，女人的身體搖動著，只是一癱沒了生氣
　　　　的肉。

女人二：媽，你說話呀！媽，你說話呀！

男人三：一隻烏鴉落在女人身邊，靜靜地等著。

男人一：又一隻烏鴉落在女人身邊，靜靜地等著。

女人三：好幾隻烏鴉落在女人身邊，靜靜地等著。

男人二：一群烏鴉落在女人身邊，靜靜地等著。

女人二：【大叫】媽！

男人二：女人的屍體躺在地上。

男人一：男孩坐在她的身邊。

男人三：一群烏鴉落在他們身邊。

女人三：它們沒有叫，只是靜靜地等著。

【一聲槍響，一陣槍響】

【麻木，在空氣中蔓延】

【燈光漸暗。女人身上的光越來越強】

【光突收】

人物：女人一 ...... 王國慶的母親，四十多歲
　　　女人二 ...... 王國慶，男孩，十三歲
　　　男人三
　　　女人三
地點：重慶，兵工廠之間的空地
時間：1967年

【音樂突起，鑼鼓喧天】

【燈光隨著男人三的描述漸起。男孩跪在女人的面前，一動不動】

男人三：整個下午，工廠裡都群情激昂。

女人三：整個下午，男孩就坐在女人身邊。

男人三：男人們都剃光了頭，女人們也都剪了短髮。

女人三：他一動不動，眼裡沒有一滴淚水。

男人三：幾千人聚在工廠的大院裡，每人手中都拿著一桿槍。人
　　　　們因為激動而漲紅了臉。

女人三：他轉過頭，那個牆洞還吐著腥紅的舌頭。

男人三：人們匆匆地走過牆角，時刻準備著迎接即將到來的戰鬥。
　　　　沒有人停下來，看一眼牆上的洞。

女人三：太陽漸漸地冷下來，落到山的那邊去了。月亮升起來。女人的臉在夜色中飄浮著，就如同天上雲層裡的模糊不清的月亮。

男人三：寂靜。

女人三：寂靜。

男人三：戰鬥開始前的寂靜。

女人三：死一般的，寂靜。

男人三：燈光暗。

【燈光漸暗】

人物：女人二 ...... 王國慶。男孩，十三歲

　　　男人二 ...... 父親，中年男人，四十多歲

　　　女人三 ...... 兒子，十五六歲

　　　男人三 ...... 王一清，四十多歲，王國慶的父親

　　　男人一 ...... 男，三十左右，兵工廠的武裝分子

　　　女人一 ...... 男，二十左右，兵工廠的武裝分子

地點：重慶郊外，荒山

時間：1967年

【突然，槍聲密集，夾雜著炮聲】

【女人二跑上舞臺。他拼命地跑著】

女人二：我沒命地跑著，子彈、炮彈就在我身邊亂飛。我多希望
　　　　能撞上，那樣，那樣我就和媽媽一樣了。我跑出了那片
　　　　沙地，我跑到小路上，我跑到山腳下，我跑到田野裡……
　　　　月亮始終跟著我，媽媽的臉就飄在我的前面……槍聲越
　　　　來越遠，聽不見了。我喘著氣，媽，媽，媽！

【女人二摔倒在舞臺上】

【男人一、男人三、女人一穿著軍裝，他們手中持著槍押著女人
三、男人二上】

男人一：晚上九點鐘左右，月亮已在中天，大地清輝一片，山林
　　　　的小路上，走著五個男人，他們都穿著軍裝。一個留著
　　　　鬍子的中年男人和兩個年輕的男人手裡端著槍，他們押
　　　　著一對父子，一個中年男人和一個十五六歲的年輕人。
　　　　他們的胳膊上戴著紅綢章，眼睛用黑布給蒙上。

男人三：【指著中年男人】你們有多少人？

男人二：四千。

男人三：槍從哪裡來的？

男人二：八五七廠換的。

男人三：八五七廠？

男人一：他們也是……

女人一：他們跟我們一邊的。

女人三：不，他們跟我們一邊的。

男人二：別説了。

女人三：爸，怕啥，是的，他們是我們一邊的。他們給我們換的
　　　　是機槍，給他們換的是步槍。

女人一：他媽的。主任，我們給騙了。

男人三：都給閉嘴，奶奶的。

男人一：靜場。

男人二：停頓。

女人一：只有腳步聲。

男人一：中年男人回過頭來，他説：

男人二：你兒子在我們這邊。

女人一：王一清盯著中年男人。

男人三：他不是我兒子。

男人二：他是我們的組長，他打仗很英勇。

男人三：【用槍指著年輕男子，對中年男人】你要是再多嘴，我
　　　　打死他，你兒子。

女人三：爸，我不怕。

男人一：靜場。

女人一：有風，樹葉沙沙地響起來。

男人二：一清。

男人一：叫王主任。

男人二：王主任，蒙著眼，我也知道你們是誰？一清，咱們也是
　　　　熟人，要不是這打仗，大家都是抬頭不見低頭見的人，
　　　　何必這麼認真呢！你這是要把我們往哪裡帶啊？

男人一：抓回去，再説。

男人二：你們怎麼對待俘虜？

男人三：不知道。

男人二：現在，人少，我們好商量的，要不，人一多，就不好辦
　　　　了。你們先放了我倆。我會報答你們的。

女人三：爸！

男人二：等仗打完了，你們廠還是要採購我們廠的輪胎的，下次來，你找我。

女人一：靜場。

女人三：沒人說話。

男人一：風過竹林，嗚嗚的，像是人哭。

男人三：【用槍指著中年男人】走，少囉嗦。

【五個男人走遠，男孩爬跑著過來】

女人二：【喊】爸！

男人三：誰？

女人一：【用槍指著男孩】站住。

女人二：爸。

男人三：你怎麼在這裡？

女人二：爸，我媽死了。

男人一：國慶啊，你別瞎說。

女人二：爸，我媽死了，就在你們的工廠外面，她要帶我去鄉下外婆家，被人用槍打死了。

男人三：甚麼時候？

女人二：今天中午。

男人三：中午？

女人二：有人用槍打的。

男人三：我知道了。

女人二：爸，我媽死了，她還在那裡呢，在你們工廠外面的沙地上。

女人一：靜場。

男人一：靜場。

男人二：靜場。

女人三：靜場。

女人二：【哭】爸。

男人三：別哭了。

【王一清看著那對父子，又看著兒子。他扯下父子眼上的黑布，拿出兩把鐵鍬，交給他們】

男人三：挖。

男人一：主任。

女人一：不是這兒。

男人三：就是這兒，挖。

男人二：挖甚麼？

男人三：坑。快點兒。

【父子倆開始挖泥】

女人二：中午，我和我媽在那裡歇著，我走不動了，熱，我媽不讓歇。就在這時候，突然有人打槍了，就一槍，我一直在那裡，全是血，爸，爸！全是血！

男人二：缺德！

男人一：少廢話，挖。

女人一：一鍬，兩鍬，三鍬⋯⋯父子倆拼命地挖著坑。突然，父親放下鐵鍬，他抬起頭。

男人一：怎麼了？

男人二：你，你們挖這坑幹甚麼？

女人三：挖。

男人二：【驚恐地】一清，你⋯⋯你別亂來，你老婆可不是我們打的。

女人一：靜場。

男人一：靜場。

男人二：求你們了！

女人三：他面無表情。爸，你別求他。

男人二：天啊，他們怎麼可以這樣！⋯⋯你們要是懲罰，就懲罰我好了！求求你們，他還小，你們放過他。

女人三：爸！

男人一：兒子拼命地挖著土，懲罰，懲罰，懲罰好了。

男人二：【跪下】求你們，殺我，別殺他，他才十五歲啊，求求你們。

【王一清手中的槍響，父親立即仆倒在地。兒子扔掉鐵鍬跑過去。】

女人三：【哭喊著】爸！

女人一：王主任，別！

男人一：主任，說好了是帶他們回廠裡。

【王一清手中的槍響，兒子仆倒在父親身上】

男人一、女人一：【喊】主任。

男人三：埋了。

【兩個男人拿起鐵鍬。王一清轉過身看著男孩】

男人三：國慶，過來，我們找你媽去。

【王一清攙起孩子的手，他們下】

【兩個男人拿著鐵鍬，怔怔地站著】

女人一：風，刮過竹林，嗚嗚地，像人在哭。

男人一：雲，遮住月亮，山坳裡一片漆黑。

女人一：遠處，火光沖天。

男人一：密集的槍聲遠遠地傳過來⋯⋯

【燈光漸暗】

人物：男人一 ...... 王國慶，二十四歲

　　　男人二 ...... 王國堅，男，三十多歲，王國慶的哥哥

　　　男人三 ...... 王一清，五十多歲，王國慶的父親

地點：重慶

時間：1978年

【激進的音樂。歡呼聲。男人二上場】

男人二：在農村待了八年，當王國慶再次回到重慶時，那是1978
　　　　年，一切早已物是人非了！

【舞臺的後面出現王國慶，他背著包，滿臉的風塵。父親出現在
舞臺前方的一角】

男人二：王國慶從別的路線回了家，他遠遠地繞過了兵工廠，因
　　　　為在他的腦海裡，母親一直就躺在那裡。

男人三：我找到她了，把她的身體擦拭乾淨，用白布包裹著，埋
　　　　進了陵園。國慶，你一直都在場的。

男人一：我只記得她的身體倒在草地上，血不停地流出來，厚厚
　　　　的灘滿一地。

男人二：整整十年。

男人一：血灘滿一地。

男人三：忘了它，國慶。

男人二：畢竟都過去了，國慶。

男人一：你們可以選擇忘記，或許強迫自己忘記，可我，不。

男人三：記著，又有甚麼意義。

男人一：【沖著王一清喊】記著，是不要讓它再發生。

男人三：停頓。

男人二：整整十年。

男人一：我與父親，我們不說一句話，就像是陌生人。

男人二：國慶。

男人一：哥。

男人二：回家吧。

男人一：他在嗎？

男人二：爸？在。

男人一：【站住】我不想回。

男人二：那你去哪裡？【稍停】要不，去我家吧。

男人三：停頓。

男人一：這座城市不屬於我，它很陌生。

男人二：王國慶與哥哥站在大街上。四下裡人來人往，人們的臉
上洋溢著喜悅，他們在慶祝新時代的到來。

男人三：王國慶抬起頭，一隻烏鴉在城市破舊的建築中艱難地飛
著，它飛得很吃力，隨時都有可能掉下來。

男人一：【低下頭】這座城市早已腐爛，破敗不堪！【冷漠地】
　　　　　呱、呱、呱！

男人二：都過去了，國慶，朝前看，人，還得活著。

男人一：你知道他是誰？

男人二：知道。

男人一：我不會饒了他的。

男人二：都十多年了。

男人一：我會親手殺了他的。

男人二：國慶。

男人一：哥，你不用說了。遠處，天很藍，江水湍急。

男人二：我想讓爸爸跟我住，他不肯。他說，他怕。

男人一：【冷笑】他怕？

男人三：我怕，我怕你媽回來了，找不到我。

【沉默。王國慶點上一根煙，抽著，吐著煙圈】

男人一：回家吧。

男人二：國慶？噢，好的。

【王國慶與哥哥走到父親王一清面前】

男人二：國慶回來了，爸。

男人三：【冷漠地】回來了！

男人一：【冷漠地】回來了。

男人二：停頓。

男人一：停頓。

男人三：停頓。就像是過了十年。

男人一：他比我想像的要蒼老許多，身體乾瘦了，背也駝了。

男人三：你長大了，國慶。【稍停】回來就好。

男人一：有啥好的。

男人三：國慶，你抽煙了？

男人一：在黑龍江，冬天，不抽煙，會死的。

【王國慶看著父親，把煙丟在地上，用腳碾踩著。轉身，下】

【燈光暗】

人物：男人一 ...... 王國慶，二十五歲

　　　男人三 ...... 王一清，五十多歲，王國慶的父親

地點：重慶，市政禮堂

時間：1979年

【燈光起，男人一站在舞臺的中央】

【夜晚，城市的聲音。嘈雜】

【男人三出在舞臺的一角】

男人三：宣判大會看上去很熱鬧，一下子判了一百多號人，誰也
　　　　記不住誰，坐在黑壓壓的人群中，王國慶感覺自己就像
　　　　是個被丟棄掉的孩子。王國慶一直閉著眼睛豎著耳朵聽
　　　　著，他生怕那個名字從自己的耳底溜走---丁建國。

男人一：丁建國----我睜開眼，努力地從臺上站著的一排人當中尋
　　　　找那個叫丁建國的男人。可他們都低著頭，我不知道哪
　　　　個是----丁建國。

男人三：丁建國，三年。

男人一：丁建國，三年？有期徒刑三年！這怎麼可能，一條命，
　　　　只判三年。

男人三：高音喇叭嗡嗡地叫著，犯人們一排一排地上場，下場。

台底下的人們繼續打著招呼、嗑著瓜子，大呼小叫一會兒，家長里短一下，就散了。

男人一：就像是做夢一樣。

男人三：空蕩蕩的禮堂裡一片狼藉，只剩下兩個男人，他們遠遠地坐著，低著頭，不說話。

男人一：下雨了，雨打在禮堂外的破舊的玻璃窗上，怦怦直響。

【急雨聲，越來越大】

男人一：王一清站起來，他走到禮堂的外面，雨越來越大。禮堂前的廣場上一個人也沒有，城市在大雨中肅默。

男人三：這城市剛剛睡醒，還不清醒。王國慶站起來，他邁不動腿，感覺那腿不是自己的。

男人一：我站在他身邊，默默地看著雨。

男人三：他站在我身邊，一言不發。

男人一：雨，很大，一切都有些模糊。

男人三：雨，很大，沒命地下著。

男人一：一隻烏鴉站在不遠處的電線上，雨水打濕了它的羽毛。它蜷縮著，一動不動。

男人三：王一清看著那只烏鴉，感覺它像隨時都會掉下來。

男人一：三年？

男人三：誤殺。

男人一：他故意的。

男人三：那個時候……

男人一：怎麼了？

男人三：也不能全怪他，所有的人都……瘋了。

男人一：這不是理由。

男人三：確實。

男人一：我不會饒了他的。

男人三：你想怎麼？

男人一：三年。

男人三：三年？

男人一：我就再等三年。

男人三：國慶，你那時候還小，你不明白，可現在你應該明白了，
　　　　這樣沒有意義。

男人一：是的，那時候我小，不明白，現在我明白了，我要殺了
　　　　他。不管怎樣！

男人三：他已經得到懲罰了。

男人一：【冷笑】三年，夠嗎？

男人三：不會有夠的時候，國慶。

男人一：他是你的同事，你知道是他，你竟然饒了他。

男人三：沉默。

男人一：沉默。

男人三：雨，一直下，就像是水倒在地上。

男人一：他們的臉沉如死水。

男人三：雨，一直下。

男人一：唔，你看那裡。

男人三：王國慶指著不遠處馬路邊上的電線杆，那上面站著一隻
烏鴉。烏鴉蜷縮著，也正看著他。甚麼意思？

男人三：沉默，只有雨聲。

男人一：沉默。那只烏鴉。

【王國慶抬起頭】

男人一：他甚麼也沒說，縮了縮脖子，徑直走進雨裡。

男人三：雨澆在我的身上，很快全身就濕透了。

男人一：破舊的白色老頭衫一下地就濕了，貼在他身上，透出他
肥贅的肉和臃腫的身子。

男人三：我努力地挺直著身體，全身都泡在雨水裡。我像是哭了，
我不想讓他看到我哭。

男人一：我看著他的身影漸漸地消融在雨中。

男人三：雨很大，全是淚水。

【王一清走向舞臺的縱深處，下】

男人一：王國慶抬起頭，雨水打在他的臉上，冰涼冰涼的。他盯
著那只烏鴉，就好像是自己站在電線杆上。這個城市的
上空，烏雲密佈，無數的雨線從夜空中掉下來，王國慶
感覺自己的身體飄在雨水中，一直在上升，上升……從
半空中打量這座城市，竟是如此的陌生。

【雨聲越來越大】

【燈光漸暗】

人物：女人二 ...... 王國慶的妻子，二十多歲

　　　男人一 ...... 王國慶，二十八歲

　　　男人三 ...... 王一清，五十多歲，王國慶的父親

　　　男人二 ...... 王國堅，三十多歲，王國慶的哥哥

　　　女人三 ...... 女，護士

地點：重慶

時間：1982年

【燈光起，鑼鼓喧天。女人三上場】

男人二：不管是甚麼時候，這個國家都一直都在慶祝。開個會，
　　　　也會慶祝好多天，就好像以前從沒開過似的。

【舞臺的後區，燈光下，坐著女人二和男人一。男人三坐在舞臺
的一角】

女人二：她二十多歲，也是知青，回到重慶就在針織廠做工人。
　　　　（直爽地）我比你小一歲。我在江西。你哪裡？

男人一：黑龍江。

女人二：夠遠的。

男人一：我自己挑的。越遠越好。

男人二：國慶是頂替我去的。

女人二：我家裡有房子，母親剛過世。

男人二：父親呢？

女人二：十多年前在武鬥中死了。

男人二：國慶……

男人一：行。

男人二：甚麼？

男人一：行，哥。我娶她。

女人二：我們結婚了。

【結婚的音樂起。舞臺中央兩把椅子。王國慶與妻子面對面坐在上面】

男人一：謝謝你。

女人二：謝甚麼？

男人一：嫁給我。

女人二：那我也得謝你，娶我。

男人一：我會爭取做一個好丈夫，好父親。可……王國慶看著妻子的臉，她臉上幸福的喜悅裡藏著幾絲疑問。

女人二：怎麼了？

男人一：我是個有仇的人。

女人二：有仇？

男人一：殺母之仇，這個仇我一定要報的，我會不惜一切代價，哪怕……

女人二：他的眼裡滿是仇恨。我不禁打了個冷顫。哦！我知道了。

【護士上，她推著一張病床到王一清面前。王一清躺了上去】

【王國慶和妻子、哥哥走過去。護士搖了搖頭】

男人三：你們……我有話要跟國慶説。

【妻子、哥哥和護士下場】

【王國慶看著父親】

男人三：國慶，你少抽煙。

男人一：當著他的面，我吸了一口煙，慢慢地吐著。

男人三：國慶，我……

男人一：説吧，我聽著呢。

男人三：那天下午，在工廠的院子裡，剛發下來的槍……他的槍
　　　　是我給的。【稍停】丁建國試的槍，是我給的。

男人一：停頓。

男人三：停頓。

男人一：王國慶看著父親，他覺得自己的腦子嗡嗡直響。

男人三：國慶？

男人一：王國慶的拳頭握得緊緊的，他甚至能聽到關節的聲響。

男人三：國慶？國慶！

男人一：王國慶盯著父親。

男人三：國慶……

男人一：王國慶看著父親挺了挺身體，爬起來，他的手僵硬地伸著，想抓住兒子。王國慶一下地躲開，他看著父親重重地摔回到床上。

男人三：國慶！

男人一：我看著他的臉一點點地扭曲起來。

男人三：國慶，我，我⋯⋯

男人一：王國慶轉過頭，看著監視儀。他的心跳越來越慢，時間也跟著慢了下來。

男人三：國慶！

男人一：他在病床上掙扎著。可我沒有看他，我只是盯著監視儀，看著他的心電波變成了直線。

【王一清掙扎了會兒，平靜下來。哥哥、妻子與護士衝上來。護士忙碌著】

男人二：爸！爸！爸！

女人二：快，快叫醫生。

女人三：醫生，醫生！

【護士跑下場】

女人二：爸，爸！國慶！國慶？

男人一：【走到台前，吸著煙】我看到母親的身體倒在草地上，血流了一地。

【燈光漸暗】

53

人物：男人一 …… 王國慶，三十三歲

女人二 …… 王國慶的妻子，三十多歲

男人二 …… 丁建國，四十多歲

男人三 …… 王國堅，男，四十多歲，王國慶的哥哥

女人一 …… 服務員

地點：重慶，家裡

上海，醫院

時間：1987年

【燈起。靜場。女人二出現在舞臺的後區】

女人二：日子一天天地過去，這註定是一個喧囂的春天！烈日炎炎，萬物凋零，這註定是一個哀痛靜默的夏天。多久了，這個世界發生的一切都與王國慶沒有關係。

【男人一上】

男人一：我只是活著。

女人二：停頓。

男人一：我開卡車，總是在開，我喜歡開，開著車在路上行駛，我就覺得我在駛向一個明確的目的地。直到那天，偶然的機會，我知道他在上海。

女人二：回來了？

男人一：啊。【看著妻子】

女人二：怎麼了？

男人一：我找到他了。

女人二：他？【吃驚地】他！

男人一：是的，丁建國，他在上海。

女人二：國慶，兒子考試成績不錯。

男人一：我們……離婚吧。

女人二：吃飯吧。

男人一：甚麼都歸你，孩子也是，只是離婚。

女人二：我做了你喜歡的紅燒肉。

男人一：我會去上海。

女人二：要米飯嗎？

男人一：他病了，住在醫院裡。

女人二：要不要辣椒？

男人一：我偷了輛吉普車，辦完事，看情況，興許我就不回來了。

女人二：上海人喜歡吃甜的。

男人一：如果我活著……我會給你們寄錢回來的。

女人二：啤酒要嗎？國慶。

男人一：苦了你了。

女人二：冰鎮的。

男人一：我對不起你，可是你不能放棄，這與你和孩子無關。

女人二：……

男人一：對不起。

女人二：我給你盛飯去。

【女人二轉身，下】

男人一：我開著吉普車去了上海。白天我會找個僻靜的地方在車裡睡一覺，晚上我才上路。我感覺自己一直被黑暗包裹著，只有車燈一直亮著，照著各種各樣的路面，大部分情況下都是泥路，塵土飛揚。我就像那塵土一樣在燈光翻滾著，從來沒有落定的時候。

【舞臺的後區，病床上，躺著丁建國】

男人一：我知道在這個世界上的某個地方，一個叫丁建國的男人還活著。我們就像是兩顆星星，一顆想逃脫，一顆想抓住，我們都失去了自己運行的軌跡，它們不會平行，總有一天會碰在一起的。只有毀滅了一顆，另一顆才有可能回到自己的軌道上去。

【王國慶走過去，拿著一把尖刀，他指著丁建國】

男人一：起來。

男人二：【爬起來】誰？

男人一：你不認識我。

男人二：是的。

男人一：可我認識你。

男人二：你要幹嗎？

男人一：殺你……二十年前，你殺了一個女人。

男人二：我沒有---

男人一：你閉嘴。

男人二：你聽我解釋。

男人一：沒這個必要。

男人二：你到底是誰？

男人一：我是她兒子。

【王國慶用尖刀刺向丁建國】

【丁建國倒在病床上】

【王國慶用床單擦拭乾淨尖刀，走向台前】

【舞臺後區照著病床的燈光暗】

男人一：我曾經無數次地想過如何殺丁建國……我把他從監獄裡
　　　　搶出來，活埋掉。我去攔截囚車，當著其他犯人的面宣
　　　　判他死刑……而這一次，我要把他殺死在病房裡。

【王國慶茫然地走著、嘮叨著】

男人一：上海的街頭很熱鬧，那家醫院也很好找。中午11點45分，
　　　　醫生與護士都去食堂打飯去了，那時的病房裡沒有人，
　　　　只有他。12點半，醫生與護士就都回來了。我只有45分
　　　　鐘的時間。我帶了蛇皮口袋、繩子、刀，好幾把刀……

我給吉普車加足了油，停在醫院的外面。如果他跟我鬥，我就在病房裡殺了他。如果他聽話，我就把他綁架到重慶，在母親的基前殺了他。

【舞臺後區照著病床的燈光漸起】

男人一：一大早，我就坐在醫院對面的餐館裡。

【女人一上場，她鋪好桌子。王國慶坐下】

男人一：現在有點菜嗎？

女人一：早餐還是午餐？

男人一：午餐。

女人一：也太早點了吧！

男人一：有沒有？

女人一：【不情願地】有。

【王國慶把點單給了服務員。她接過去，端上來幾盤菜和兩瓶啤酒】

男人一：菜吃在嘴裡，卻沒有味道，我像是失去了味覺。

女人一：【雙臂環抱在胸前，看著王國慶】神經病。

男人一：人們在我面前飄來飄去的。

男人一：【看了看手錶】幾點了？

女人一：11點了。【嘟噥著】你不是戴錶了嗎？

男人一：結帳。

女人一：付錢的時候，他的手一直在抖。

男人一：她有些緊張地看著我。

女人一：這人有毛病。

男人一：她會不會報警？我走進醫院，找個拐角的地方蹲下來，前兩天我就在這裡踩過點。我把一把刀別在腰上，手裡拿著一把，用報紙包著。蛇皮口袋裡還有一把長的刀。繩子、膠帶、榔頭……一切準備就緒。

女人一：王國慶坐在地上，渾身是汗。

男人一：怎麼這麼熱？才五月份。

女人一：王國慶一直盯著病房的門。

男人一：那裡靜悄悄的，沒有人進出。

女人一：11點30分，王國慶站起來，他站得有些不穩，差點兒摔倒。於是，他狠狠地扇了自己一個耳光。

男人一：耳光很響，我的頭嗡嗡的，好像全身都腫脹起來。醫生與護士都拿著飯盒有説有笑地走了。

女人一：他的腿機械地向前邁著。前方100米的地方，就是丁建國的病房。

男人一：透過窗戶我能看到裡面有人走動。

女人一：王國慶看了一下手錶，11點40分。

男人一：我僵立在臺階下，我能看到輸液架和上面掛著的輸液瓶。

女人一：11點41分。

男人一：病房的窗簾被掀了起來。

女人一：王國慶趕忙轉身急急地離開。他重又回到拐角的地方。

男人一：媽的！

女人一：11點43分。

男人一：窗簾還在動。媽的，是風。

女人一：11點44分。他深吸了兩口氣，敲了敲自己的頭。11點
　　　　45分。他站起來迅速地跑過去。院子裡很安靜，甚至有
　　　　一兩聲鳥鳴。臺階有些滑，他一個踉蹌，差點摔倒，手
　　　　中的蛇皮口袋掉在地上，哐噹一聲。他趕忙拾起口袋，
　　　　把手中的報紙扔掉，一腳就踹開了房門。

【王國慶向舞臺後方的病床衝過去】

女人一：王國慶撲向病床，一把掀開被子。床上沒有人。

男人一：我的頭一下子麻了起來。床上沒人！

女人一：他像一頭被關在籠子裡的獅子似的，在病房裡四下裡找
　　　　尋著。

男人一：沒人，沒人，一個人也沒有。

女人一：王國慶翻看著病床上的吊牌，丁建國，沒錯。輸液瓶上
　　　　寫的名字，是丁建國，沒錯。

男人一：王國慶來回地走著。

女人一：11點55分。

男人一：門外，有人影飄過，悄無聲息。

女人一：王國慶衝出病房，他站在院子裡，長長地舒了一口氣。

男人一：剛才一直屏著氣，像是沒有呼吸過。

女人一：王國慶一直站在那裡，不停地哆嗦著。

男人一：我控制不住自己，渾身發冷，就像是抖篩子一樣，不停地抖。

女人一：12點20分。護士走進病房。

男人一：王國慶轉身，急急地離開醫院。

【王國慶在舞臺上急急地奔走著】

女人一：中午，陽光很烈。

男人一：街上，全是冷漠的面孔。

女人一：王國慶感覺自己就像是在人群之中飄浮著。

【王國慶突然停住，他立在舞臺的前方】

【男人三拿著電話上場】

【清脆的電話鈴聲】

【舞臺後方的病床燈亮。丁建國從病床上起身，他下床接電話】

男人三：丁建國？

男人二：是的。

男人三：我是王國堅。

男人三：王國堅？

男人二：王一清的兒子，大兒子。

男人二：你好。

男人三：你在上海？

男人二：……

男人三：我弟弟去了上海。

男人二：……

男人三：他知道你住的醫院，他去找你了。

男人二：……

男人三：他一直在找你……你……躲躲吧。

【王國堅掛上電話】

【誇大的電話被掛斷的聲音。丁建國有些失魂落魄地掛上電話，轉身跑下場】

男人一：哥？！哥！

【王國堅看著弟弟，他面無表情】

男人一：為甚麼？

【王國慶手中的刀一下地掉落在地上】

男人二：呱、呱、呱！

男人一：一隻烏鴉一邊叫著一邊飛著，它飛得很快。

男人二：它很快就消失在上海的夜色之中。

男人一：1987年6月的上海，竟然如此的冷。

【燈光暗】

人物：男人一 ...... 王國慶，四十六歲

　　　男人二 ...... 丁立明，丁建國的兒子、上海法官，三十歲左右

　　　男人三

　　　女人一

　　　女人二

　　　女人三

地點：上海外灘

時間：2000年

【燈光起】

【放煙花的聲音與光影】

【男人三、女人一、女人二和女人三在舞臺上行走著】

【丁立明在他們中間穿行，他的臉上浮著笑】

【王國慶出現在舞臺的一角，看著他】

男人二：2000年的最後一夜，千禧夜！一千年才一次，上海，

　　　　外灘，全是人。

男人一：煙花在空中炸開，稍縱即逝。花火映著人們密集的仰

　　　　視著的臉，夜幕下的城市就像到了高潮似的呻吟著、

　　　　哆嗦著。

男人二：站在人群之中，雖然被擠得東倒西歪，王國慶看著人們的歡呼與莫名的興奮。隔著人群，他只盯著一個人。

男人一：隔著人群，我一直盯著他，他的臉上，意氣風發、躊躇滿志。

男人二：丁立明在人群中穿行，就像是一條在春水暢遊的參鰷魚，能留在上海，做名法官，這是他一輩子的夢想。

男人一：一個人可以消失十年，蹤跡全無。可總會有些蛛絲馬跡。

【王國慶圍著丁立明走著，審視著他】

男人一：十幾年後，我沒找到丁建國，可我卻找到了他的兒子，丁立明。

男人二：一個法官。

男人一：一條參鰷魚。

男人二：參鰷魚？

男人一：一種在水中急行的小魚，他們有一條頭魚，不管對錯，所有的魚群都會跟著頭魚。我給你一個期限，也是給我的。

男人二：期限？

男人一：是的。我母親死的那年，我十三歲。所以，你有十三年的機會。

男人二：十三年？

男人一：十三年。如果過了十三年，你還是個好人，我就放了你。

男人二：好人？【笑】甚麼是好人？

男人一：適用於大多數人制定的標準---法律。

男人二：法律？

男人一：十三年內，只要你不違法，我就放過你。

男人二：你有甚麼權利？

男人一：權利？【笑】你父親給我的。

男人二：我父親？

男人一：他叫丁建國。

男人二：丁建國，那個我叫他父親的男人，在遙遠的天際邊，飄
　　　　浮著。

【男人三、女人一、女人二和女人三，下場】

男人二：遠遠的，那個男人，他看人的樣子好奇怪，他立在人群
　　　　中，卻與人們沒有關係。

男人一：其餘的人都像是不存在似的，只有你和我，一個人對一
　　　　個人。

男人二：煙花放完了，人群又在黑暗中蠕動。那麼多人，誰是好
　　　　人，誰又是壞人？

男人一：糞坑裡的蛆蟲。

男人二：城市，喘著粗氣。

男人一：燈光漸暗。

男人二：黑暗，就是一塊狗皮膏藥，它可以掩蓋傷疤，卻掩蓋不了疼痛。

【王國慶和丁立明盯著對方】

男人一：這些人在歡呼甚麼？

男人二：跨入新千年，我們早就體無完膚。

【燈光漸暗】

人物：男人一 ...... 王國慶，五十四歲

　　　男人二 ...... 丁立明

　　　男人三 ...... 丁立明的堂妹夫

　　　女人一 ...... 丁立明的妻子

　　　女人二 ...... 丁立明的堂妹

　　　女人三 ...... 丁立明的女兒、丁立明的情人

地點：上海、北京

時間：2008年

【燈光起】

【王國慶穿著風衣，靜靜地站立。他有些瑟縮發抖，

不禁縮了縮身體】

【其他人站在舞臺的一角，他們看著他，與他形成一種對峙】

男人三：寂靜！

男人二：怦、怦、怦……

女人一：寂靜！

男人二：怦、怦、怦……

女人二：寂靜！

男人二：怦、怦、怦……

女人一：寂靜！

男人二：怦、怦、怦！寂靜得能聽到心跳。

男人三：王國慶立在宣傳欄前，那裡一點也找不出他一個星期前
　　　　曾經貼過抗議書的蹤跡。

【王國慶聲嘶力竭地大聲叫，他蜷縮著身體，蹲了下來。可是卻發
不出一點聲音】

男人三：寂靜！

女人一：寂靜！

女人二：寂靜！

女人三：寂靜！

男人二：寂靜！沒有人理，沒有人！

男人三：石沉大海。

女人一：鴉雀無聲。

女人二：悄然無息。

女人三：無聲無息。

男人二：……

男人三：事情發生了，可就像是沒有發生一樣。

男人二：意料之外，卻又是意料之中。

男人三：王國慶早知如此。

男人二：他就是參鯀魚群中的一條魚，絕不會是那條頭魚。

【王國慶慢慢地站起來】

男人一：我覺得我就是一隻站在電線杆上的烏鴉。我拼命地叫
　　　　著，卻沒人聽到我的聲音。

【烏鴉張大嘴，叫了起來】

男人二：呱、呱、呱！

【越來越多城市的聲音：人聲、汽車聲、嘈雜而模糊】

【聲音越來越大，排山倒海，蓋過烏鴉的聲音】

【聲音越來越小，寂靜】

【烏鴉張大嘴，卻發不出聲響】

男人二：……

男人三：寂靜！

女人一：寂靜！

女人二：寂靜！

女人三：寂靜！

男人一：那麼大的城市，死了一樣。我只能聽到我的心跳。它非
　　　　常有節奏，那是催我前行的戰鼓。

【遠雷】

男人三：雷聲，遠遠的滾過來。

女人三：城市，煩燥的很。

女人一：空氣，悶熱的很。

男人一：我走在街上，汗珠不停地滾落下來。周圍的人都有些模

糊，形影綽綽，從身邊無聲地滑過。我不停地走著，渾身卻充滿了鬥志。

【王國慶急急地走著】

女人二：我裡面有人。

男人一：我知道他是誰。我跑了起來，像是有著使不完的力氣。

女人二：我上頭有人。

男人一：我知道他是誰。

女人二：你贏不了。

男人一：現在只是開始。我跑著。

女人二：你算了吧，何苦呢。蒼蠅不叮無縫的蛋。

男人一：我就是要找出那條縫。我為甚麼要跟你做生意？就是在等他出手。

女人二：等他？誰？

女人三：烏鴉飛了起來。

男人三：下雨了。

男人一：他果然出手了。他不是個好人，這就夠了。我就像是拿到了通緝令，該我行動了。

女人三：烏鴉飛了。

男人一：我是你黑夜裡潛行的影子。可當我舉起刀的時候，刀面泛出了光亮，於是，我便沒有了影子。

女人三：下雨了，桃花都開了。

男人一：我買了四輛車，換了不同的司機，來跟蹤。

男人三：老闆？

男人一：跟著他。

男人二：老婆，我回來了。

女人一：下班了？累吧？

男人二：累，沒完沒了的官司。

女人二：老闆？

男人一：跟著他……這不是他家？

女人二：老闆？

男人一：你先開回去。

女人二：你呢？

男人一：我自己回。

男人二：老婆，我來了。

女人三：誰是你老婆。急死了，才來。進來，快點兒。

男人二：就你知道急。

男人一：我蹲在門口，看著手錶，秒針一點點地過去，分針，然
　　　　後是時針。兩個小時。這狗娘養的。一炮時間還挺長。

男人三：老闆？

男人一：照舊。

男人二：老婆，女兒的家長會開了沒有啊？

女人一：開了，你還知道管啊。

男人二：忙。

女人一：就你忙。

男人二：明天晚上我不回來了。

女人一：又不回來？

男人二：有官司。

女人二：老闆，盯著他？

男人一：是。

男人二：親愛的，我來了。

女人三：怎麼這麼晚？

男人二：我開女兒的家長會。

女人三：你？

男人二：好，不提了。

女人三：那今晚你不許走。

男人二：好，我不走。

【王國慶走到舞臺中央，他猶豫了好久，敲門。丁立明的情人開門】

女人三：你找誰？

男人一：噢，我是送快遞的。

女人三：【上下打量著王國慶】快遞？

男人一：這是603嗎？

女人三：不是，這是1603。

男人一：對不起，看錯了。

【丁立明的情人關上門】

男人二：誰啊？

女人三：送快遞的，送錯了。

男人一：【打電話】喂……我要舉報法官丁立明……

【王國慶掛上電話】

男人三：他有三處價值千萬的房產，他的老婆沒有工作，他還包
　　　　養了一個情人……

男人一：這些都不致命……於是，我去了北京。

【烏鴉張大嘴，卻發不出聲響】

男人二：……

男人三：寂靜！

女人一：寂靜！

女人二：寂靜！

女人三：寂靜！

【眾人給王國慶脫去破舊的衣服，換上西裝、皮鞋與風衣，他拎
上皮包，顯得神采奕奕】

男人一：我不是一個上訪者，也不是去擊鼓鳴冤。

女人一：國家信訪辦。

男人三：姓名：王國慶。

女人二：國家政法委。

男人三：性別：男。

女人一：國家最高人民法院。

男人三：年齡：五十六。

女人二：天安門廣場。

男人三：民族：漢。

男人一：我要舉報法官丁立明！

男人二：冬天的北京，風吹在臉上就像是刀割一樣的疼。

男人一：風扯著我的頭髮，在四周肆無忌憚地嚎叫著。偌大的天
安門廣場，空空蕩蕩的，只有遠處的霓虹在不安地閃爍
著。一隻凍死的烏鴉硬挺挺地躺在水泥地上，它的爪子
捲曲著，像是想抓住些甚麼。可是，只有寒風。

女人一：一個清潔工走過去，她把烏鴉的屍體掃進簸箕裡。

男人一：我被那個女人掃進簸箕裡，然後被倒進了垃圾箱。我僵
硬的身體砸在洋皮桶裡，哐噹一聲。

女人一：那聲響瞬間就消散在寒風中，無聲無息。

女人三：我曾經飛翔過的天空，一直陰沉著。

女人二：一個員警走過來。

男人三：喂，幹甚麼呢？

男人一：不幹甚麼。

男人三：那你在這裡幹甚麼？

男人一：我？

男人三：證件。

【王國慶木然地掏出證件，遞給員警，員警看著】

男人三：姓名。

男人一：王國慶。

男人三：性別。

男人一：男。

男人三：年齡。

男人一：五十六。

男人三：包裡有甚麼？

男人一：文件。

男人三：打開。

【員警看了看王國慶的公事包，把證件還給他。離開】

男人三：走，走啦！

男人一：知道了。

女人二：一個中年男人走過來。

男人二：看升旗呢？還有六個小時呢。

男人一：我不看。

男人二：不看？那我勸你離開。

男人一：……

男人二：可以嗎？

男人一：我這就走。

男人二：識相點兒，這裡不是你想待就待的地方。

男人一：我現在真想擊鼓鳴冤了，可是，我的鼓，在哪兒呢？

【遠遠地，傳來密集的鼓聲。鼓聲越來越響】

【燈光漸暗】

人物：男人一 ...... 王國慶，五十六歲

　　　男人二 ...... 丁立明，四十歲左右

　　　男人三 ...... 廣場舞者

　　　女人三 ...... 廣場舞者

　　　女人一 ...... 女孩

　　　女人二

地點：上海

時間：2010年

【燈起】

【舞臺的兩側坐著一個女人和一個男人。他們穿著一樣的花襯

衫、白褲子、黑皮鞋】

【兩個人對視著】

男人三：黃昏，太陽還沒落下。街角公園的長椅上，坐著一個男

　　　　人和一個女人。即便都是老人，但看不出他們真實的年

　　　　齡。他們都打扮得一絲不苟。

【女人最終站起來，她試著扭了扭腰，走了走舞步。又覺得不好

意思，停了下來】

男人三：男人看著她，他輕聲地問：新來的？

女人三：不是。你？

男人三：也不是。

女人三：沒見過你啊。

男人三：我也是。

女人三：你會跳？

男人三：不會。

女人三：我也是。

男人三：不，其實你跳得挺好。

女人三：不好意思。

男人三：我也是。

女人三：女人看著男人，她說不出更多的話。靜場。

男人三：靜場。

女人三：他看了看手錶。

【男人三看了看手錶】

男人三：她用手理了理早已順貼的頭髮，轉過頭去。

女人三：西邊的天空早已緋紅。陽光還在高樓的玻璃幕裡掙扎，
　　　　閃著刺眼的金色的光。他看著我？

男人三：男人看著女人。

女人三：女人轉過頭來。他是在看著我。【笑】我們來早了。

男人三：沒事。

女人三：是的。沒事。

【另外兩男兩女上場，他們穿著相同的服裝】

【男人與女人旋即放鬆起來】

【一個男人手裡拿著放音機。他一摁按鍵，吵鬧的、通俗的口水歌音樂突然響起。隨著音樂，三個男人和三個女人開始跳著廣場舞。舞步簡單而粗俗。看上去乏味而單調，但是跳舞的人樂在其中】

【一個男人慢慢地人群中跳出來，他停下來，若有所思地看著這群人。男人脫掉身上的花襯衫，他是王國慶】

男人一：王國慶看著這些廣場舞者，他們曾是科長、處長、局
　　　　長，曾是藍領、白領、金領，曾是教授、教師、職員！
　　　　可現在，他們都是廣場舞者。

【一個女人慢慢地人群中跳出來，她停下來，看著這群人。女人脫掉身上的花襯衫。她是女孩】

男人一：一個女孩衝到街角，她怒氣沖沖地衝著這群人叫起來。

女人一：【叉著腰】別跳了，吵死了。

男人一：音樂和舞蹈繼續，沒人理她。

女人一：【叉著腰】你們還有沒有腦子，都這麼大歲數了啊。

男人一：音樂和舞蹈繼續，沒人理她。

女人一：【叉著腰】你們這是擾民，懂嗎？我要去告你們，你們
　　　　也有家庭，也有孩子，你們也不想想，別人還要生活
　　　　呢！你們講不講道理啊，你們還是人嗎？活了這麼大歲

數，怎麼還是這樣的自私自利，你們是畜生嗎？說你們呢！罵的就是你們！天啊，這是怎麼了！你們難道是白癡嗎？白癡，白癡。

【一個男人走到放音機前，他動了一個按鈕，音樂聲旋即更大起來】

男人一：女孩看著他們。

【女孩看著這群人，她逐漸地平靜下來，她慢慢地又穿上花襯衫。跟著人們跳起來】

男人一：王國慶看著這些人，他感到有些害怕。他既渴望成為他們，又怕成為他們。

【音樂漸收。跳舞的人脫下花襯衫。他們在舞臺上走著，王國慶穿梭在他們中間】

男人一：王國慶在大街上走著，他感覺有只老鷹一直在他的頭頂盤旋著。於是，他買了能錄影的眼鏡，制訂著自己的計劃。一年、兩年、三年，他不著急，要想打到狐狸，你就得比狐狸更狡猾。這是一個人與一個人的戰爭，他不指望群體，但他可以利用群體。

【三個男人醉醺醺地東倒西歪地走著】

男人三：立明，沒事，張律師買單，小妞不錯，你自己挑。

男人二：他小子，學乖了，那官司哪有這麼容易！這裡安全嗎？

男人一：沒事，老據點了。

男人二：【語不倫次】出了事⋯⋯找你⋯⋯

男人一：她們賣，我們買，願買願賣，公平交易，能出甚麼事？

男人三：小費，你照給，張律師會給你要回來的。

男人二：他小子，現在倒大方了……

【三個女人打扮成護士、員警和學生，上。她們搔姿弄首地從男人面前走過。三個男人色眼迷迷地看著】

男人一：學生妹不錯，我要了。

男人二：就你這老牛，還想吃嫩草。當心牙口。

男人一：立明，你放心，我咬得動。

男人三：立明，你挑，護士與員警，我都喜歡。

男人二：每天看的都是女員警，倒胃口了，我挑護士。

【眾人下。王國慶立住】

男人一：唱歌兩小時，吃飯三小時，開房四小時……

【丁立明上。他遠遠地看著王國慶。王國慶轉身看著他。他們似曾相識。丁立明走向王國慶，卻與他擦肩而過，下。王國慶轉身，看著他下場】

男人一：這一年，我跟蹤他，我們有許多次面對面地走過，我以為他看到了我，可是我們總是擦肩而過。

【照著王國慶的燈光暗】

人物：男人一 ...... 王國慶，五十八歲

　　　男人二 ...... 丁立明，四十歲左右

　　　男人三

　　　女人一

　　　女人二

　　　女人三

地點：上海某殯儀館

時間：2012年

【燈起】

【哀樂響起。舞臺的中央，男人三與三個女人背立著。他們黑衣黑衫】

【丁立明立在舞臺的前面，垂手肅立。王國慶上】

男人一：中午，即便陽光鮮亮，殯儀館裡依舊毫無生氣。除了哀樂流動的旋律，只有偶爾爆發出的聲嘶力竭的嚎啕大哭顯得有些活力。我花了五十元買了一隻花圈，走進了這位死者的大廳，他是誰我並不認識，可我知道他的女婿叫丁立明，一個我跟蹤了十二年的法官。

【王國慶走上前，他握住丁立明的手】

男人一：節哀！

男人二：謝謝。

男人一：他握住我的手，手很有力，也很溫暖，他的眼裡滿是感
　　　　激。我盯住他，他也盯著我。他面頰紅潤，斯斯文文，
　　　　歲月對他不薄，可他的眼角分明滑過一些懷疑與狡黠。

男人二：這個人有些面熟，像是在哪裡見過。

男人一：我得走開，不能讓他懷疑。保重。

【王國慶走開】

男人二：謝謝。

男人一：他不認識我。可我卻認識他。我站到人群的背後，靜靜
　　　　地盯著他。就像是藏在雲層背後的鷹，靜靜地盯著樹叉
　　　　上的烏鴉。整整半個小時，我就這麼看著他，這感覺真
　　　　的很奇妙。

男人二：安靜。

男人一：只是哀樂在我的目光中流淌。

男人二：我最不喜歡殯儀館，它讓一切都變得毫無意義。

男人一：殯儀館真是一個好地方，讓人看破紅塵。

男人二：甚麼官職、地位，甚麼女色、金錢，都是過眼雲煙。

男人一：跟了他那麼久，證據也收集到那麼多。一件件都是鐵證，
　　　　但都不能扳倒他。

男人二：人生不過如此，不如及時行樂。

男人一：無所謂，我等著，我相信，他是管不住自己小弟弟的。

男人二：這群人看上去很傷心。

男人一：遺像上的男人笑著，有些詭異。

男人二：他們掛著臉，流著淚，為他，還是為他們自己。停頓。

男人一：停頓。

【丁立明突然轉身看著王國慶，他們對視著。王國慶艱難地擠出絲笑容。人群散去】

男人一：【上前】保重。

男人二：謝謝。

男人一：再見。

男人二：再見。

【丁立明目送著王國慶下場。哀樂漸收】

【燈光漸暗】

人物：男人一 ...... 王國慶，六十歲
　　　男人二 ...... 丁立明，四十歲左右
　　　女人二 ...... 妓女
　　　男人三 ...... 保安以及丁建國
地點：上海某會所
時間：2014年

【黑暗中，傳來男人粗喘的聲音】

男人三：黑暗！甚麼都看不見。

男人二：黑暗！可甚麼都可以感受得到。一次一次的撞擊，停止
　　　　不了的瘋狂的撞擊，每一次撞擊都把這個男人引向更加
　　　　快樂的頂點。

男人三：黑暗！甚麼都看不見。

男人二：黑暗！被我一次一次地撞開，我看見了整個世界。

男人三：黑暗！擠壓著一切。

男人二：黑暗！讓一切都快速地膨脹，越來越大，越來越強，在
　　　　快樂的頂點，我變成了煙花。

男人三：煙花在夜空中炸開，璀璨無比。

男人二：我照亮了夜空。

男人三：黑暗，沒了。

男人二：我看到我扭曲變形的臉。

【燈光漸起。丁立明與女護士整理著衣衫】

男人三：男人真是一種奇怪的動物，花了那麼長時間去追逐，只
　　　　是幾秒鐘，就從空中摔回到地上。

男人二：我覺得我就是----

女人二：一頭公豬。

男人二：……？

女人二：哥，你真行。

男人二：是嗎？

女人二：人家都快不行了。

男人二：到底是行還是不行？

女人二：討厭，你行人家才不行嘛。

男人二：下次還找你。

女人二：哥，你真狠，翻臉就不認人了。

男人二：我認你就行。

【王國慶戴著眼鏡上場，他走到丁立明與女護士身邊，圍著他們
走著，看著】

男人一：對，就是這，你放慢點兒。

男人三：你到底丟了甚麼？

男人一：一個公事包。

男人三：你可以報警。

男人一：你真逗，我來這裡找小姐，你讓我報警？

男人三：你也真是的，是不是一下地爽歪了，就……【笑】以後可要當心點兒。

男人一：你再重播一下，就是這兒。

【王國慶圍著丁立明與女護士轉著，丁立明挽著女護士的手】

男人一：對，這一段你放慢點兒，我看看，是，就是這個男人，我看到過他，那時候我的手裡應該還拿著包的。

男人三：你都看了好多遍了。

男人一：好了，看樣子是找不到了。

男人三：找小姐你帶包幹甚麼？帶個小包就行了。

男人一：小包？

男人三：【笑】你懂的。

男人一：喲，你們呀，真壞。

男人三：我們，還能有你們壞啊。我們保安，只能看錄影，不像你們，看都不用看，辦，就行。

【丁立明和女護士下場】

【王國慶指著丁立明下去的方向，轉身看著男人三】

男人一：打蛇要打七寸。

男人三：他是我兒子。

男人一：我不管你躲在哪兒，他，就是你的七寸。

【丁建國下場】

【王國慶摘下眼鏡，看了看】

男人一：可以錄影的眼鏡，真他媽是好東西。接下來，該我
　　　　出腳了。

【燈光漸暗】

人物：男人一 ...... 王國慶，六十歲

男人二 ...... 丁建國，七十歲

男人三

女人一

女人二

女人三

地點：網路

時間：2014年

【燈光起。三男三女出現在舞臺上】

【敲擊鍵盤的聲音、網路裡的各種聲音】

男人三：網路真是個好地方！

女人一：每個符號的背後，都是人的身影。

女人二：隨機取個綽號，你想罵誰就罵誰。罵了，誰也不會知道
你是誰？

女人三：那些有名有姓的人要是落在你的口中，你想怎麼咬就怎
麼咬？只要他有血有肉，你就總能找到下口的地方。

女人一：你就是一條藏在黑暗深處隨時可以竄出來狂咬的瘋狗，
你從不用擔心，因為叫聲會引來人們的圍觀，人們喜歡

看狗咬人，只要那個被咬的人不是自己。

女人二：他們更希望看人咬狗，可沒幾個人會樂意出來與一隻狗
　　　　對咬的，否則，就會引來更多人的圍觀。

女人三：其結果就是：人被咬得遍體鱗傷，狗卻因此樂此不疲，
　　　　狂吠不已。

女人一：只要被咬的不是自己，沒有人會關心那些竄出來咬人的，
　　　　到底是條狗，還是頭豬。

女人二：他們藏在黑暗深處，磨尖了自己的牙齒，隨時準備衝出
　　　　來，咬。

女人三：咬，瘋狂地咬。

女人一：他們頂著人的名號，幹著豬狗的勾當，咬。

男人三：她竟然是小三。

女人一：咬。

女人二：她竟然穿成這樣。

女人三：咬。

男人二：他竟然吸毒。

女人一：咬。

男人三：他竟然升遷。

女人一：咬。

女人二：他的工資？

女人三：咬。

男人二：他竟然上餐館？

女人一：咬。

男人三：他竟然買了房子。

女人一：咬。

女人二：他一上午上了兩次廁所。

女人三：咬。

男人二：他竟然是個人。

女人一：咬。

男人三：他是誰？

女人一：咬。

女人二：他是誰？

女人三：咬死他。

男人二：他是誰？

女人一：咬死他是誰。

女人一：咬。

男人三：咬。

女人一：咬。

女人二：咬。

女人三：咬。

男人二：咬。

女人一：咬。

男 女：咬。

男人一：我註冊了一個帳號，隨便起了個名字，然後把剪輯好
　　　　的視頻放在網路上，讓幾個朋友轉發一下。於是，咬
　　　　聲四起。

【各種狗叫與廝咬的聲音，越來越大】

男人一：半個小時。

女人一：王國慶坐在電腦面前，看著轉載量直線攀升。

男人二：一個小時。

女人二：已經能聞到血腥味。

男人三：兩個小時。

女人三：狗咬狗，狗咬人，人咬狗，人咬人……

男人二：法官嫖娼，轉。

女人一：法官買春，轉。

男人三：醜聞，轉。

女人二：刺激，轉。

女人三：天啦，轉。

男人二：好，轉。

女人一：靠，轉。

男人三：轉。

女人二：轉。

女人三：轉。

男人二：人渣。

女人一：罪犯。

男人三：殺了他。

女人二：殺了他。

女人三：殺了他。

男人一：他們比我還憤怒。

女人一：狗，總比人顯得憤怒。

男人二：三個小時之後。

男人三：王國慶刪了錄影，登出了帳號。

女人一：風暴已經形成。

男人二：五個小時之後。

女人二：各位觀眾，我們剛剛收到的新聞，法官買春被網路
　　　　曝光……

男人二：七個小時之後。

女人三：法官丁立明嫖娼視頻被網路瘋傳……

男人二：第二天。

女人一：請問你是王國慶嗎？

男人二：市紀委、市高院對丁立明等五名法官集體嫖娼事件進
　　　　行調查……

女人二：你不怕被報復嗎？

男人二：市委公佈法官嫖娼案處理結果……

女人三：你為甚麼要報仇？

男人三：法官嫖娼案輿情分析……

女人一：你是怎樣拿到第一手資料的。

男人二：法官嫖娼案事件始末……

男人三：一個星期之後，這些只是網路裡的文字符號，沒有人會記得住。

女人一：人們依舊生活。

女人二：狗們依舊張著嘴。

女人三：咬。

男人三：咬。

女人一：咬。

女人二：咬。

【突然，電話鈴聲。男人二打電話，王國慶接聽手機】

男人一：喂！你好！喂？

男人二：我是丁建國。我在香港，你來吧，我等你！

女人一：雨越來越大。

女人二：燈光漸暗。

【雨聲，雨聲】

【燈光漸暗】

人物：男人一 ...... 王國慶，六十歲

男人二 ...... 丁建國，七十歲

男人三

女人一

女人二

女人三

地點：香港

時間：2014年

【燈光起】

【雨聲，越大越大】

【男人三和女人一、女人二、女人三都穿著雨衣，把自己裹得嚴嚴實實的。他們靜立在舞臺的中央】

女人一：都是因為陽光，我才從海面上掙脫出來。我在空氣中快樂地飛舞，不斷地上升，溫度越來越低，我撞到了你。

女人二：於是便沒有了你，也沒有我。

女人三：我繼續上升。越來越多的水滴，細小的水滴。我們繼續上升。

女人一：我們碰撞著，聚在一起。

女人二：那就是我，我是一片雲，在夜空中堆積。

女人三：越來越厚。

女人一：越來越冷。

女人二：雨滴在雲層裡凝聚。

女人三：我在你的身體裡凝聚。

女人二：我托不住你。

女人一：我掙脫出雲層，叫著喊著，快樂地砸向地面。

女人二：我們一起奔向地面。

女人三：滑過高樓、樹梢，奔向地面。

女人一：雨像是下不完似的！

女人二：往下，往下！

女人三：砸在地上，砸在人的身上。四分五裂。

女人二：王國慶聽著窗外的雨聲，密密麻麻，像是敲在他心上。

男人一：我盯著牆上的鐘，看著秒針一點一點地往前走著。可是
　　　　分針像是從來不動似的。王國慶看了一下手機，凌晨三
　　　　點四十七分。

女人三：窗外傳來低沉的歌聲。聽不清，遠遠的，像雷般地滾過
　　　　來，又在城市的夜空中遠去。

女人二：雨季過後的草原，野牛群奔過。

【男人三哼著歌，是那種進行曲式的歌聲】

男人三：嗯嗯嗯……！

女人三：王國慶坐起來，黑暗包裹著他。他能聽到血液流動的聲音。流過他的臉頰、胸膛，甚至髮梢。

【燈光下，王國慶突然出現，他光著身子站著】

女人一：一個閃電無端地亮起來，黑夜在窗外張著嘴，像是要吞噬掉一切。

男人一：我從床上爬起來，腳落在地上，像是踩在彈簧上。

女人二：王國慶一瘸一拐地走到窗前。

女人三：窗外，漆黑一片。只有遠處偶爾亮起的閃，閃出厚厚的雲層，遙遠的很。

男人三：嗯嗯嗯……！

男人三：王國慶走到衛生間，地上濕嘰嘰的，他的腳掌蜷縮著，立在地面上，涼得很。

女人二：他打開燈。燈竟然亮了。

女人一：燈亮的一瞬間，他不禁晃了晃，有些站不穩，甚麼都看不清。

女人三：王國慶擰開水龍頭，把水澆在臉上，順勢喝了許多水。

女人二：水很涼，他覺得清醒了許多。

女人一：涼水順著食道跌落到他的胃裡，把浮在空中的他拉回到了地面。

女人二：他打開洗澡用的水龍頭，水一下地噴出來。

男人一：水澆在我的身上，我不禁一個激靈。

男人三：2014年7月的香港。中環的一家酒店。凌晨四點十一分。冷水澆在王國慶的身上，他猛地打了一個激靈。

女人一：內褲⋯⋯汗衫⋯⋯西褲⋯⋯襯衫⋯⋯西裝⋯⋯襪子⋯⋯領帶⋯⋯皮鞋⋯⋯手錶⋯⋯

女人二：凌晨四點三十二分。

女人一：王國慶穿好衣服。

女人二：他再次檢查了手提包。

女人三：榔頭⋯⋯菜刀⋯⋯砍刀⋯⋯匕首⋯⋯蛇皮袋⋯⋯繩子⋯⋯頭套⋯⋯通行證⋯⋯火車票⋯⋯錢包。

女人二：他抽出一張人民幣，上面的人正咧著嘴笑著。

男人三：哈哈哈哈哈哈！

女人二：門卡⋯⋯門⋯⋯電梯裡一個人也沒有。

女人一：四點四十一分。

女人三：叮⋯⋯

女人二：前臺的服務員抬起頭，睡眼惺忪。

男人一：你好。

女人一：出去？！

男人一：是的。

女人一：當心！

男人一：再見。

男人三：大廳裡空蕩蕩的。王國慶用力推開玻璃門。

女人二：風把他的領帶刮了起來，貼在他的臉上。

女人三：雨無情地砸在他的身上。

男人一：媽的，沒帶傘。

男人三：本來就不需要傘。

男人一：王國慶一頭紮進雨水裡，雨水順著他的頭髮、臉頰、頸
　　　　脖，流進他的身體裡。

【王國慶疾走著，男人三和女人一、女人二、女人三，他們把雨
帽戴上，跟著他、圍著他。甚至拉著他，他艱難地走著】

女人一：王國慶在雨中走著。

女人二：王國慶在中環的大街上走著。

女人三：王國慶在人群中走著。

女人一：雨，越來越大，瘋狂地砸著地面、人們。

女人二：大街上全是人，黑壓壓地。

女人三：人們在唱著歌。

男人三：嗯嗯嗯……！

女人一：人們靜靜地坐著。

女人二：人們靜靜地坐在街上。

女人三：人們靜靜地坐在雨水中。

男人三：嗯嗯嗯……！

女人一：王國慶在人群中走著。

女人二：他踩到人們的衣服。

女人三：沒有人動。

女人一：他的提包碰到人們的身體。

女人二：沒有人動。

女人三：他的腳狠狠地踢到人的身上。他摔倒在地，仆倒在人的
身上。

【王國慶摔倒在地上】

女人一：沒有人動。

男人三：嗯嗯嗯……！

男人一：對不起。

女人二：沒有人動。

女人三：王國慶從人堆裡爬起來。

【王國慶爬起來】

女人一：人們看著前方，遠遠的，那個黑魆魆的建築魔鬼似的蹲
在那裡。上面被貼著各種各樣的標語，滑稽得很。王國
慶覺得在甚麼地方見過。

女人二：王國慶在人群中艱難地走著。

女人三：人們直直地坐著，直直地看著遠方。

男人三：嗯嗯嗯……！

女人一：雨水密集地打在王國慶的臉上。

女人二：他就像在雨水中飄浮著。

女人三：順著水流被沖向遙遠的地方。

男人三：嗯嗯嗯……！

女人一：王國慶艱難地離開了人群。

女人二：街上靜得很。

女人三：凌晨四點五十九分。

男人三：在雨聲之中，王國慶能聽到自己的腳步聲。很急。

【王國慶擺脫眾人的拉扯，他跑了起來。男人三和女人一、女人
二、女人三慢慢地走到舞臺的盡頭】

【王國慶拼命地跑著】

女人一：海堤。

女人二：冷冰冰地立在那裡。

女人三：海水。

女人一：就像是煮沸了一樣，翻滾著。

女人二：黑漆漆的，翻滾著。

女人三：泛起白沫，淒慘得很。

男人三：凌晨五點，風雨之中，王國慶在香港的街頭跑著。

女人一：城市很巨大，無聲地立著。

女人二：雲層掩過高樓，一切都變得虛幻起來。

女人三：雨聲、風聲、浪聲，遙遠的歌聲。

男人三：嗯嗯嗯……！

【燈光下，丁建國突然出現，他穿著西裝，默默地站著。王國慶在他的面前立住】

女人三：雨嘩嘩地下著。

【疾雨聲】

男人三：他們默默地對視著。

男人一：雨水在他的臉上肆虐地流淌，他眯起眼，看著我。

男人二：雨水砸在他的臉上，他瞪著眼，看著我。

男人一：他的嘴緊緊地閉著，我看不到他的目光。他這麼老了！

女人三：雨聲、風聲、浪聲，遙遠的歌聲。

女人一：噓！

女人二：寂靜。

女人三：王國慶能聽到自己的心跳聲。

男人二：我是丁建國。

男人三：王國慶的手緊緊地攥住提包。

女人一：天，很藍。

男人二：我想忘掉……那時候……

女人二：沒有風。

男人二：人們失去了理智，所有的人，我只是他們當中的一個。

女人三：陽光很毒。

男人二：我不知道我做了甚麼，卻……殺了你的母親。

男人三：烏鴉在空中盤旋。

男人二：我只是一個年輕人，我只是相信，盲目地相信，我相信人多的力量，那麼多人，肯定是對的，沒有人會去思考，思考是多麼的可笑而多餘，大家都這麼幹，這樣是對的。我們都變得瘋狂、兇殘、心狠手辣……

女人一：女人的臉，慘白。

男人二：對不起。我知道你一直在找我，你父親、你哥哥、你妻子、你兒子……我知道你，你的一切。

女人二：血從她的胸口流出來，汨汨的流出來，流在了草地上。

男人二：從重慶到上海，從上海到北京。

女人三：草，很綠。

男人二：你毀了我的兒子。

男人一：他罪有應得。

男人三：他們默默地對視著。

【丁建國突然從懷裡掏出一把手槍，直指著王國慶，王國慶後退了一步】

女人一：雨，越來越大。

男人二：我一直在逃，你從不放過。

女人二：風，刮在臉上，生疼的很。

男人二：那不是他的錯。丁立明，我兒子。

女人三：海水撞擊著海堤，轟隆隆地被撞得粉碎。

女人一：分不清是海水還是雨水。

【丁建國慢慢地把槍頭倒轉過來】

男人二：喏，你肯定沒帶槍。給你。

【王國慶看著丁建國，他慢慢地接過手槍，直指著丁建國】

男人二：對不起。

女人一：手槍原來這麼重。

男人二：今年我七十歲，我逃了四十多年，是該了結了。

女人二：雨水打在王國慶的手上，濺起了水花，消散在了風中。

男人二：早該了結了。

男人一：雨水打在他的臉上，他一直眯著眼。雨水在他的臉上肆
　　　　虐著，就像是淚水。

男人二：雨水順著他花白的頭髮往下淌著。

男人一：他是誰？

男人二：丁建國。

男人一：丁建國是誰？

女人一：王國慶的手顫抖著。

男人一：這槍怎麼這麼重？我的臉熱熱的，是淚，我怎麼哭了？
　　　　我當著他的面，哭了？

【王國慶看著丁建國，他慢慢地放下手槍。丁建國吃驚地看著他】

男人一：雨水從他的鼻尖上滴落，長長地。他哭甚麼？

男人二：【伸出手】我不該讓你來承擔殺人的罪責，我自己來。

女人一：王國慶看著丁建國，他伸出的手不停地在顫抖著。

男人二：我清楚那槍裡子彈已經上膛。其實，也沒甚麼。

【王國慶把槍慢慢地遞向丁建國】

女人一：王國慶突然抬起手臂，把槍扔了出去。槍落在海水裡，
　　　　無聲無息。

【王國慶把槍扔了出去】

男人三：寂靜。

女人一：風，越刮越緊。

男人三：寂靜。

女人二：雨，越下越大。

男人三：寂靜。

女人三：海水撞擊著堤岸。

男人三：香港，中環，海邊。雨中。王國慶、丁建國，他們面對
　　　　面靜靜地站著。

【王國慶轉身離開，他急急地走著。男人三和女人一、女人二、
女人三跟著他】

【丁建國癱坐在地上，照著他的燈暗】

女人二：街道上一個人也沒有。

女人三：天邊泛起了魚肚白。

女人一：城市漸漸地清晰起來。

女人二：雨，甚麼時候停了。

女人三：風，甚麼時候停了。

女人一：王國慶急急地走著。

男人一：我抬起頭，雲沒了，只剩下空空的天，蒼白的很。

男人三：王國慶突然摔倒了。

【王國慶突然摔倒】

女人一：一隻烏鴉。那只烏鴉。

女人二：地上有一隻烏鴉。

女人三：地上有一隻死烏鴉。

男人三：它僵硬地躺在那裡。

女人一：一個清潔工走過去。

女人二：你好，你沒事吧？

男人一：沒事。

女人一：她把烏鴉掃進簸箕裡。

男人一：我被那個女人掃進簸箕裡，然後被倒進了垃圾箱。我僵硬的身體砸在洋皮桶裡，哐噹一聲。

女人一：你看，真可憐。

男人一：是的，好可憐。

女人二：王國慶爬起來。

【王國慶爬起來】

男人一：人呢？人群呢？

女人二：散了。

男人一：那麼多人，散了？

女人二：可不就散了。活著，本來就不容易，別盡跟著瞎起哄啊！

女人三：清潔工走遠了。

女人一：大街上空無一人。

女人二：王國慶站在大街上，他覺得很冷。

男人一：真冷。

女人二：你這是要去哪兒？

男人一：誰？

女人三：你。

男人一：我？

女人一：是的，你，王國慶。

女人二：寂靜。

男人一：我不知道。

女人三：寂靜。

男人三：王國慶像是聽到了一聲槍響。

男人一：我像是聽到了槍響。

【巨大的槍響】

【燈光急暗】

人物：**男人一**

　　　　男人二

　　　　男人三

　　　　女人一

　　　　女人二

　　　　女人三

地點：**劇場**

時間：**現時**

【燈光起】

【人們立在舞臺的中央，他們黑衣黑褲】

男人三：【誇張地】有一群烏鴉，它們口渴了，到處找水喝。

男人二：烏鴉們看見一個瓶子，瓶子裡有水。

男人一：可是瓶子裡水不多，瓶口又小，烏鴉們喝不著水，怎麼辦呢？

女人一：怎麼辦呢？

女人二：怎麼辦呢？

女人三：怎麼辦呢？

男人一：烏鴉們渴死了。

男人二：我們渴死在碎石子上面。

男人三：我要是一個人，就好了。【看了看手錶】晚上，九點三十分。劇場。大幕落下，演出結束。觀眾退場。

【燈光漸暗】

- 全劇完 -

"A motley crew may come together lightly, but with time, repulsion is inevitable - cordial but never close."

— Guan Zhong, *Guanzi*

Character: Man 2 – Crow
Location: Theatre
Time: Now

(*Lights up*)

Man 2
stands centre stage, dressed in black. He glances at his watch.

Man 2 (*looks up*)
Seven-thirty. Evening. Theatre. Audience arrives. Curtains up. Performance begins. A crow. It's thirsty. Looking all over for water. Sees a bottle. Water inside, but not much. The bottle's neck is small. Can't get to the water. What to do? I see lots of pebbles nearby. I've an idea. I'll put the pebbles into the bottle one by one. The water level rises. Ha. I can drink. Actually, I can put other things in. Twigs, egg shells, baby crows. I can dig a hole in the ground to tilt the bottle. I'll be able to reach the water too. I can even find a stalk from the wheat fields and suck the water up. Or I can simply push the bottle over, water'll come out... (Stares at the audience.) Having drunk the water, I fly away.

(*Blackout*)

Character: Man 1 - Wang Guoqing, around 60 years old
            Man 3
Location: A hotel in Hong Kong
Time: 2014

(*Darkness. Anxious, rapid gasping interspersed with sleep talk*)

(*Rain. Thunder. Lightning*)

(*Man 3 stands quietly.*)

Man 3: 2014. July. Midnight. Hong Kong. Hotel. Outside. Pouring down. Splattering hard. Lightning, cuts through the window into the room; the white sheets look exceptionally ominous. Wrapped in these sheets, Wang Guoqing twists and squirms. The bed is squeaking and groaning, about to fall apart. Thunder rumbles. Splatter. Squeak. Rumble. Splatter... squeak... rumble...

(*The clatter from the downpour fades. Thunder vanishes. Lightning disappears.*)

Man 3: Splatter... squeak... rumble... splatt?... Squeak... rumb?... Squeak? Squeak... squee? (*He quiets down gradually.*)

(*Man 1 twists and turns on the bed, punctuated by anxious gasps and pants. Chewing and moving his lips, he is mumbling unintelligibly in his sleep. Suddenly, he makes a piercing scream.*)

Man 1: Crow? Crow. Crow! Ma? Ma! Crow! Ma, ma! (*Screams*) Ma!

Man 3: Wang Guoqing yanks the covers off, leaping upright, gasping for air.

Man 1: I stand on the bare floors. Gasping. One a.m. says the clock on the wall. In the mirror stands a man. Can't see him clearly. He's naked. He's not in great shape – gaunt, wiry. Like an exhausted monkey. I need some food. Right, instant noodles. Walk past the bathroom. The floor is cold. Barefoot. Fuck.

Man 3: Splaaatter... splaaatter...

Man 1: I shudder. Fuck.

(*The flush of a toilet*)

Man 3: No light in the bathroom.

Man 1: Fuck.

Man 3: Pause.

Man 1: Two mice scutter across. Into my foot. Fuck.

Man 3: Squeak... squeak...

Man 1: I dig out two snack sausages from my backpack. And a penknife.

Man 3: Wang Guoqing goes to the sofa with his finds. He turns on the table lamp and examines them. He cuts them open carefully with his knife.

(*Wang Guoqing chews the pieces of snack sausage he has cut with his eyes closed.*)

Man 3: Wang Guoqing chews on the snack sausage. (*Chews*)

Man 1: I'll chop him into eight pieces, then bit by bit carve out little chunks of flesh, tiny chunks - bite size. Put one into the month. Chew slowly. (*Chews*) A bit sweet. A bit chewy. Chilled. Like chewing raw beef. (*Chews*) Tissues, tendons, the stench of blood...

Man 3: Chewing on the snack sausage, Wang Guoqing goes to the window. He pulls up the blinds. Hong Kong under the cloak of night is drifting in the downpour. Like a woman who's just climaxed, lazing wantonly, moaning in post-coital bliss.

Man 1: Chewing on the snack sausage, I look out of the window. In the glass, the city's highrises jab into my dull yellow body, churning up and down.

(*Lightning. Thunder*)

Man 3: Wang Guoqing watches his reflection in the window. That blurry, gnarled, warped body. It becomes sharp and sinister in the lightning. Like countless glittering needles, threads of rain pierce through his body, straight and slant.

Man 1: As if I've vanished. Only the black night.

Man 3: Outside, twenty floors down is the ground. On the ground is cement. Soggy, connected, it supports the city. Lots of metal barriers on the ground. A dark and dense crowd sits fenced in by these barriers. The crowd extends into the distance, further than the eye can see. It wraps this city, silent in the night.

Man 1: Silence.

Man 3: Rain, knocks on their heads, faces, bodies. Runs down their hair, cheeks, necks, soaking them. They hold their heads high, looking ahead. Silence.

Man 1: Silence.

Man 3: One, two, three...

Man 1: A crowd, the whole square, full of people.

Man 3: They're bathing in the rain. A force flows with the rain.

Man 1: Spreading.

Man 3: Hong Kong, soggy, bobbing up and down in the rain.

(*Bang! Wang Guoqing jumps.*)

Man 1: A crow hits the window. Scares me.

Man 3: Following the glass and along with the rain, the crow falls and falls... falling into the dark and dense crowd.

Man 1: I close the blinds.

Man 3: Wang Guoqing closes the blinds.

Man 1: I chew on the snack sausage, listening to the sound of my own chewing.

Man 3: Wang Guoqing chews on the snack sausage, he can hear the sound of his own chewing. (*Chews*)

(*Man 1 and Man 3 chew with their eyes close.*)

(*Lights fade to blackout.*)

Character: Man 1 - Crow, arsenal worker

Man 2 - Crow, Ding Jianguo (secretary of the arsenal, age 23)

Man 3 - Crow, neem tree, Wang Yiqing (father of Wang Guoqing, in his 40s)

Woman 3 - Crow, weed, male arsenal worker

Woman 1 - mother of Wang Guoqing, in her 40s

Woman 2 - Wang Guoqing, a 13-year-old boy

Location: The clearing between the arsenals, Chongqing

Time: 1967

(*Darkness. A crow croaks, lonely and sad*)

(*A murder of crows croak, cacophonous*)

　　Man 3: A crow on the tree.

　　Man 2: Croak!

　　Woman 3: Two crows on the tree.

　　Man 1, Man 2: Croak!

　　Man 3: Three crows on the tree.

　　Man 1, Man 2, Woman 3: Croak!

　　Man 2: Lots of crows on the tree.

(*Silence*)

　　Man 3: Pause.

　　Woman 3: Silence.

Man 2: The sun's voice is clear.

Man 1: Tsi-tsi-tsi...

Man 3: All toasty on the body.

Woman 3: The crow pauses on the branch. He opens his beaks, croaks with all his might, but not a sound comes out.

(*Man 2 opens his mouth with all his might, croaking silently.*)

Man 1: Tsi-tsi-tsi...

Man 3: The leaves are all curled up, lifeless, withered.

Woman 3: Branches reach over the arsenal's wall – proud, extremely so. It's a grey-white cement brick wall. Bullet marks all over. Bullets scraped the cement, exposing red bricks underneath. Like a body covered with wounds, teeth bearing in a snarling mouth. The wall stands tall, separating two worlds. Posters and signs all over – recently stuck on. Ravaged by the sun, wind and bullets, they're faded and worn. A gapping hole in the wall, recently torn. A brick's snapped, half poking out of this hole. Like a dog's tongue, blood red, nakedly lolling right there.

Man 3: The tree grows in the courtyard. The trunk's thick, full of cracks blasted open by bullets – pale and pallid, howling continuously. Sap oozed out from these cracks has curdled, they hang there like falling teardrops.

Woman 3: Weed grows under the tree. No one's tended to them for a long time. They grow furiously, panting triumphantly under the sun.

Man 3: One weed, leaves, stem, roots, life, full to the brim, crystal clear.

(*Woman 3 is a weed.*)

Woman 3: My leaves are covered with soft dense hair. It can feel the movement of the air, the caress of the wind. Ah! (*Moans*)... My stem's wrapped in a thin coat. It straps my body tight. Ah! (*Moans*)... My roots reach into the soil, down there its moist and cool, I can suck to my delight. Ah! (*Moans*)...

Man 3: The sun! The savage sun.

(*Man 2 opens his mouth with all his might, croaking silently.*)

Man 1: Tsi-tsi-tsi...

Man 3: Lots of them, lots of them weed.

Woman 3: I don't know where the leaves are, or the stem, or the roots. Just lots, lots of them, lots of them weed, blurry, undefined.

Man 3: The crowd on the streets, pushing and shoving, making a racket. Chongqing, Shanghai, Hong Kong.

Woman 3: They're talking, they're shouting, I can't hear well.

Man 3: A person, a man, a young man in military uniform. He stands under the tree...

Woman 3: A tree. Leaves, branches, roots, full of life.

(*Man 3 is a tree.*)

Man 3: I'm gulping and gulping big mouthfuls of the water underground. Sweet. (*Moans in pleasure, savouring the moment, then startled*)... I can't breathe the moisture in the air. My leaves shrivel, it hurts. (*Spasms*)... My skin cracks, that damned sun...

(*Man 2 opens his mouth with all his might, croaking silently.*)

Man 1: Tsi-tsi-tsi...

Man 3: I reach my arms beyond the wall. Wind, ruffles my leaves, my shrivelled leaves. The sun's everywhere, that damned sun...

(*Man 2 opens his mouth with all his might, croaking silently.*)

Man 1: Tsi-tsi-tsi...

Woman 3: On the branches perch lots of crows.

Man 3: On my shoulders perch lots of crows. I shrug my shoulders, the crows take flight.

Man 2: Croak, croak, croak!

Woman 3: The crows return to the branches.

Man 3: The crows return to my shoulders.

(*Man 2 opens his mouth with all his might, croaking silently.*)

Man 3: I can see that clearing. The sun scorching the ground, steamy with vapour. The ground's contorting in the vapour, seems to be two persons...

Woman 3: Two persons. A middle-aged woman grap ping onto a boy's hand. They're walking rapidly.

(*Woman 1 and Woman 2 enter.*)

Woman 1: I'm holding your hand, walking rapidly.

Woman 2: I can't move anymore, Ma.

Woman 1: C'mon.

Woman 2: Ma, I really can't move anymore.

Woman 3: The woman and the boy are both wearing white shirts. Snow white. So others can tell that they don't belong to any fraction.

Woman 2: Ma, I'm hot. Can I take my clothes off?

Woman 1: No. Guoqing, just hang on a little more. They don't hurt anyone in white.

Woman 3: The woman's carrying a bamboo basket. It has some clothes and a few buns, and a bottle of water. It's a hospital drip bottle. It still got the label. But it holds boiled water now. A few pieces of rice cake bobs in the water.

Man 3: So the water'd have a taste.

Woman 2: Ma, I can't, I really can't move.

Woman 1: Guoqing, you're being naughty. What did I just say at home?

Woman 2: We'll rest when we get to gran's in the afternoon. Listen to Mama on the way.

Woman 1: That's right. Let's go.

Man 3: It's all sand. Very wide, stretching

into the distant, can't see no end. This is the clearing between two arsenals. Normally, they share this. On this end of the sand, they make tanks. On the other end, in the distant, they make cannons. Before, this place is full of tanks and cannons. Tanks leaning on cannons. Cannons resting on tanks. From afar, it's impossible to separate tanks from cannons. Lots, lots of them, blurry, undefined. Three days ago, the tanks were dragged back into the factory. Only the cannons remained. Two days ago, the cannons were all dragged back into the factory too. Nothing's left. Empty, this large stretch of land. Other than a few patches where weeds grow because water has pooled. There's nothing. Last night, bang, bang! Gunshots were heard all night. From the arsenal that makes cannons. It only stopped at dawn.

Man 2: The sun's venomous. The sand's scorching.

Man 1: Tsi-tsi-tsi...

Woman 3: The boy walks barefoot. The scalding sand makes him dance, back and forth, onto a patch of grass in the middle of the clearing.

Woman 2: Ma, I can't walk. Hot.

Woman 1: We'll rest a little.

Woman 2: Ma, I'm thirsty.

(*The Woman gives the Boy the water bottle. He gobbles it down.*)

Woman 1: Don't drink it all. We'll still need...

Woman 3: The woman turns the bottle upside down. A few drops fall onto the grass. They disappear in no time.

Woman 1: See, you've drunk it all. We've still got a long way to go, but we won't have any water.

Woman 2: Ma, words on the wall.

Woman 1: All the same.

Woman 2: (*recognising the characters*)... the gun fires, to the battlefield...! A tree, ma!

Woman 1: Neem. Bitter.

Woman 2: Ma, I don't want to go to the countryside.

Woman 1: Be good.

Woman 2: Why ain't Brother going?

Woman 1: He's got school.

Woman 2: He's not. He's fighting. Him and Papa are fighting.

Woman 1: No.

Woman 2: They're fighting. I saw them, beating people up. Papa does it. Brother too. Papa beats up those with Brother. Brother beats up those with Papa. They're not on the same side.

Woman 1: Nonsense... (*Beat*) That's why we're going to the countryside.

Woman 2: I don't wanna.

Woman 1: Be good.

Woman 2: A tree, ma!

Woman 3: She looks at the tree, silently.

Man 3: The sun's venomous.

Man 2: Tsi-tsi-tsi...

Woman 3: Leaves are shrivelled.

Man 3: My shoulders hurt.

Woman 3: He stands beneath the tree. A young man in a white shirt.

Man 1: The young man in a white shirt stands beneath me. Leaning on me. A gun in his hand. A new gun.

(*Man 2 plays around with the gun. Takes aim.*)

Man 1: Jianguo, this ain't bad.

Man 3: They came this morning. We exchanged them from Factory 857.

Man 1: Exchanged?

Man 3: A cannon for a hundred automatic. We exchanged sixty odd cannons. They know their maths. They're fighting too? On our side. They're four thousand plus, we've got six and more. Together, we're like ten thousand.

Man 1: Ten thousand?

Man 3: They've got lots too.

Woman 3: Everyone gets a gun. Plenty of bullets. Shoot away.

Man 3: Bunch of mofos, wanna attack us? We'll them some colour, so they know what we're.

Man 1: Not that bad?

Man 3: What, who doesn't know how to shoot? Back then I... those mofos, attacked us all night.

Woman 3: Command says, boys like to play with guns, it's good to get some practice. No big deal.

Man 1: Revolution isn't buying dinner for friends. It's violent when one class overthrows another.

Man 2: This is the people's war. We have to win.

Man 3: Jianguo's right. This is the people's war.

Woman 3: Ding Jianguo walks over to the wall. I move an old chair over.

Man 2: When I stand on this, I can reach that hole in the wall.

Man 1: That's risky. Watch out for their attack.

Man 3: Lunchtime, they're all napping.

Woman 3: What can you see?

Man 2: Nothing? No, someone's out there!

Man 1: (*nervously*) What? Jianguo. Get back down, it's too dangerous.

Woman 3: What can you see?

Man 2: A woman, a child.

Woman 3: Woman? Child?

Man 3: The woman's standing. The child's sitting.

Woman 3: What're they doing? That's strange.

Woman 2: Ma, what's there over the wall?

Woman 1: Your Papa's factory.

Woman 2: Papa's fighting.

Woman 1: Let's go.

Woman 2: Ma, I want to stop a bit longer. The sand's hot, my feet hurt.

Woman 1: Lazy bean. Come, I'll carry you.

Woman 3: The woman bends down, getting ready to carry the boy.

Man 1: The sky's frightfully blue. Not a hint of cloud.

Woman 3: The woman puts the bottle back into the basket.

Man 1: Breeze - a hint of breeze - ruffles the woman's hair, lifting it.

Woman 3: The fine hairs on my leaves are swaying.

Man 3: My leaves shudder, painfully, with difficulty.

Man 1: Lots of people are walking over.

Woman 3: There are actually people on the clearing out there.

Man 1: Who're they?

Man 3: Who cares? Asking for trouble.

Man 1: A whole morning. No movement at all. They're probably going to attack.

Man 3: We've got to get ready.

Woman 3: All shifts have been cancelled. Everyone's armed.

Man 1: A few ran away.

Man 3: Bastards, fuck.

Man 2: This is a good gun.

Man 3: Try it.

Man 2: Try it?

Man 3: How'd you know without trying?

Man 1: You've been a soldier.

Man 3: In North Korea. If you've never killed with it, you'd never know how good it is. Take aim, pull the trigger, fire. That's it.

Man 1: It's that simple.

Woman 3: You've to train the whole factory. We've never fired guns before. We don't even know how to pull the trigger.

Man 2: It's that simple?

Woman 1: What hit me in the chest? I heard a slight sound. What is it? It burrows into my body. What's happening? Guoqing, let's go. We can't stay here. What's that sound? Gunshot? Guoqing, run...

(*A loud gunshot. The Woman falls. The Boy is paralysed with fear.*)

Man 2: Good aim.

Man 3: Great.

Man 1: You fired?

Woman 3: How's that?

Man 2: Nothing.

Man 1: You really fired, Jianguo?

Man 3: He jumps down from the chair.

Man 2: I jump down from the chair.

Woman 3: You did it, Jianguo. Let me see.

Man 2: Nothing to see.

Man 1: He pushes the chair over.

Man 2: I push the chair over.

Woman 3: The chair falls on my body. My leaves are crashed, my stem snapped. Hurts.

Man 3: The shot shook the crows into the air.

Man 2: Croak, croak, croak!

Man 3: The shot made me shudder. The crows flew from my body. My leaves fall, drifting and spinning onto the sand. Scorching. It hurts.

Woman 2: (*Bawling*) Ma! Ma! Ma!

Man 1: The woman falls to the ground. Blood gushes out from her chest.

Woman 2: Ma, what's happening to you? What's happening? Ma, you're bleeding. I can't stop it, ma! Ma!

Woman 3: 1967. A day in July. Midday. Chongqing.

A clearing between two arsenals.

Man 1: Sky, intensely blue.

Man 2: No wind.

Man 2: The sun's brutal.

Man 3: Crows circling in the sky.

Man 2: I drink a mouthful of water. My hands won't stop shaking. Fuck, what an aim.

Man 1: I think I can hear crying.

Man 2: No.

Man 1: (*listening intently*) Right, no.

Woman 3: It's the crow.

Man 3: It's the crow.

Man 2: What peace and quiet.

(*The Boy sits on the ground, looking at the Woman, crying and shouting.*)

Woman 2: Ma, what's happening? Ma! Wake up. I'm scared. Scared!

Man 1: The woman's face. White as a sheet.

Man 2: Blood gushes from her chest, relentless, onto the patch of grass.

Woman 3: Grass, intensely green. I'm jealous. When can I be like that? Nourished by water under the midday sun, even if it's blood.

Man 3: My leaf that's fallen, shrivelled on the

ground, wilted, like a dead man's face, lifeless.

Man 1: The woman's face. Not a sign of life.

Man 2: The boy pushes the woman. Her body rolls, a lump of lifeless flesh.

Woman 2: Ma, say something! Ma, say something!

Man 3: A crow swoops down next to the woman, waiting silently.

Man 1: Another crow swoops down next to the woman, waiting silently.

Woman 3: A handful of crows swoop down next to the woman, waiting silently.

Man 2: A murder of crows swoop down next to the woman, waiting silently.

Woman 2: (*shouts*) Ma!

Man 2: The woman's body lies on the ground.

Man 1: The boy sits next to her.

Man 3: A murder of crows swoop down next to them.

Woman 3: They make no noise, just waiting silently.

(*A gunshot. A round of firing*)

(*Numbness spreads in the air.*)

(*Light fades, but the beam on the Woman is getting brighter.*)

(*Blackout*)

Character: Woman 1 – mother of Wang Guoqing, in
            her 40s
            Woman 2 – Wang Guoqing, a 13-year-old boy
            Man 3
            Woman 3
Location: The clearing between the arsenals,
          Chongqing
Time: 1967

(*Music starts abruptly. Cacophonous*)

(*The lighting grows brighter following Man 3's
narration. The Boy kneels in front of the Woman,
motionless.*)

Man 3: The whole afternoon, emotions are boiling
over at the factory.

Woman 3: The whole afternoon, the boy sits by
the woman.

Man 3: The men have shaved their heads, the
women bobbed their hair.

Woman 3: He stays catatonic, not a drop of tear
in his eyes.

Man 3: Thousands gathered in the factory's court
yard, each with a gun in their hand. Their faces
are painted red by excitement.

Woman 3: He turns his head. The hole in the wall
is still poking out its blood-red tongue.

Man 3: They hurry past the wall's corner, alert and ready for the upcoming battle. Nobody stops to glance at the hole in the wall.

Woman 3: The sun cools down gradually, setting over the other side of the hills. The moon rises. The woman's face hovers in the colour of the night, like the blurry moon shrouded in layers of cloud.

Man 3: Silence.

Woman 3: Silence.

Man 3: The silence before a battle.

Woman 3: Deathlike silence.

Man 3: Lights dim.

(*Lights fade to blackout.*)

Character: Woman 2 – Wang Guoqing, a 13-year-old boy
Man 2 – father, in his 40s
Woman 3 – son, age 15 or 16
Man 3 – Wang Yiqing, Guoqing's father,
in his 40s
Man 1 – militant from the arsenal,
in his 30s
Woman 1 – male militant from the arsenal,
in his 20s

Location: A heath in rural Chongqing

Time: 1967

(Suddenly, flurries of gunshots interspersed with the loud crack of cannons)

(Woman 2 runs onto the stage. Running desperately.)

Woman 2: I run with all my might. Bullets, cannons zoom past me. I so wish they'd hit me, so, so I'd be like ma. I run from the sandy ground, onto a path, to the foot of a hill, to the fields... The moon's always following me, ma's face drifts ahead of me... Gunshots further and further away. Can't hear them anymore. I pant, ma, ma, ma!

(Woman 2 falls over.)

(Armed and dressed in military uniform, Man 1, Man 3 and Woman 1 escort Woman 3 and Man 2 onto the stage.)

Man 1: Around nine p.m. The moon's high, illumi nating the land. In a hillside path, five men are walking. They're wearing military uniform. A

middle-aged man with a beard and two younger men
each hold a gun in their hand, escorting a father
and his son - a middle-aged man and a lad about
fifteen or sixty. They're wearing a red armband.
They're blindfolded with a black cloth.

Man 3: (*points at the middle-aged man*) How many
are you?

Man 2: Four thousand.

Man 3: Where did the gun come from?

Man 2: Factory 857.

Man 3: 857?

Man 1: They're also...

Woman 1: They're on our side.

Woman 3: No, they're on our side.

Man 2: Enough.

Woman 3: Pa, what's there to fear? Yes, they're
on our side. They gave us machine guns, but they
gave them rifles.

Woman 1: Fuck. Boss, we've been short changed.

Man 3: Shut up, all of you, mofos.

Man 1: Silence.

Man 2: Pause.

Woman 1: Only footsteps.

Man 1: The middle-aged man turns around, he says:

Man 2: Your son is on our side.

Woman 1: Wang Yiqing stares at the middle-aged man.

Man 3: He's not my son.

Man 2: He's our unit leader. He fought bravely.

Man 3: (*points his gun at the younger man and addresses the middle-aged man*) If you don't shut up, I'll kill him - your son.

Woman 3: Pa, I'm not afraid.

Man 1: Silence.

Woman 1: There's a breeze. The leaves shuffle.

Man 2: Yiqing.

Man 1: Leader Wang.

Man 2: Leader Wang, blindfolded, I still know who you are. Yiqing, we know each other well. If not for this battle, we'd be seeing each other day in day out. Why take this so seriously? Where are you taking us?

Man 1: Back. Then we'll see.

Man 2: What do you do to captives?

Man 3: Don't know.

Man 2: Right now, just a few of us, we can work something out. If there are more, it'd be hard. Let us go, we'll pay you back.

Woman 3: Pa!

Man 2: When this is over, your factory still has to come to us for our tires. Next time, come to me.

Woman 1: Silence.

Woman 3: No one speaks.

Man 1: A gust of wind cuts through the bamboo forest. Moaning. Like sobs.

Man 3: (*aims his gun at the middle-aged man*) Walk, shut your mouth.

(*The five men walk into the distance. The Boy half runs half crawls on.*)

Woman 2: (*shouts*) Pa!

Man 3: Who's there?

Woman 1: (*aims at the Boy*) Stop there.

Woman 2: Pa.

Man 3: How come you're here?

Woman 2: Pa, my ma's dead.

Man 1: Guoqing, that's no joke.

Woman 2: Pa, my ma's dead. Right outside your factory. She was taking me to the countryside, to gran's. She got shot.

Man 3: When was this?

Woman 2: Midday today.

Man 3: Midday?

Woman 2: Someone shot her.

Man 3: Right.

Woman 2: Pa, my ma's dead. She's still there. On the sand outside your factory.

Woman 1: Silence.

Man 1: Silence.

Man 2: Silence.

Woman 1: Silence.

Woman 2: (*cries*) Pa.

Man 3: Don't cry.

(*Wang Yiqing looks at his captives - the father and son, and then at his son. He pulls the blindfold from the father's and hands them two shovels.*)

Man 3: Dig.

Man 1: Leader.

Woman 1: Not here.

Man 3: Yes. Here. Dig.

Man 2: Dig for what?

Man 3: Hole. Be quick about it.

(*The father and son start to dig.*)

Woman 2: Midday, me and my ma were resting there. I couldn't walk no more. Too hot. My ma wouldn't let me stop. Just then, someone fired. Just once. I was there all along. Blood everywhere, pa, pa! Blood everywhere!

Man 2: Despicable!

Man 1: Shut up. Dig.

Woman 1: One, two, three... the father and son dig with all their might. Suddenly, the father puts down the shovel and looks up.

Man 1: What now?

Man 2: Wh...what do you want this for?

Woman 3: Dig.

Man 2: (*petrified*) Yiqing, don't... don't get it wrong. Your wife wasn't shot by us.

Woman 1: Silence.

Man 1: Silence.

Man 2: I beg you!

Woman 3: His face's blank. Pa, stop begging him.

Man 2: God, how could they?... If you want blood, take mine! I beg you, he's young, let him go.

Woman 3: Pa!

Man 1: The son digs with all his might. Blood, blood, blood.

Man 2: (*kneels*) I beg you. Kill me. Not him. He's only fifteen. I beg you.

(*Wang Yiqing's gun cracks. The father falls over. The son throws his shovel away and leaps over.*)

Woman 3: (*sobbing*) Pa!

Woman 1: Leader Wang, no!

Man 1: Leader, we said we'd take them back to the factory.

(*Wang Yiqing's gun makes another crack. The son falls on his father.*)

Man 1, Woman 1: (*shouts*) Leader!

Man 3: Bury them.

(*The two men pick up the shovels. Wang Yiqing turns around to look at the Boy.*)

Man 3: Guoqing, come, we'll go find your ma.

(*Wang Yiqing takes the Boy's hand. They exit together.*)

(*The two men stand in a trance, shovels in hand.*)

Woman 1: Wind, cuts through the bamboo forest. Moaning. Like sobs.

Man 1: Cloud, covers up the moon. The col is in darkness.

Woman 1: In the distance, fire paints the sky.

Man 1: Intense gunshots drift closer from afar...

(*Lights fade to blackout.*)

Character: Man 1 - Wang Guoqing, age 24
Man 2 - Wang Guojian, Guoqing's brother, in his 30s
Man 3 - Wang Yiqing, Guoqing's father, in his 50s
Location: Chongqing
Time: 1978

(*Rousing music. Cheers. Man 2 enters.*)

Man 2: Eight years in the countryside. When Wang Guoqing returns to Chongqing, it's 1978. Everything's changed!

(*Wang Guoqing appears upstage. He carries a rucksack, his face worn from travels. His father appears in a corner downstage.*)

Man 2: Wang Guoqing comes home on a different route. He detours far from the arsenal. Because in his mind, his mother's still lying there.

Man 3: I found her. I wiped her body clean, wrapped her in white cloth and buried her in her grave. Guoqing, you were there all along.

Man 1: I can only remember her body on the grass. The blood wouldn't stop. Thick and sticky all over the ground.

Man 2: Ten whole years.

Man 1: Blood all over the ground.

Man 3: Forget it, Guoqing.

Man 2: It's in the past, Guoqing.

Man 1: You can choose to forget, or force yourself to forget. But I - can't.

Man 3: What's the point remembering?

Man 1: (*shouting at Wang Yiqing*) Remember, so it won't happen again.

Man 3: Pause.

Man 2: Ten whole years.

Man 1: Me and father. We don't speak. Like strangers.

Man 2: Guoqing.

Man 1: Brother.

Man 2: Go home.

Man 1: He's there?

Man 2: Pa? Yeah.

Man 1: (*stands still*) I don't want to.

Man 2: Where'd you go then? (*Beat*) Erm, what about my place?

Man 2: Pause.

Man 1: This city doesn't belong to me. It's alien.

Man 2: Wang Guoqing and his brother stand on the street. It's bustling. Everyone looks joyful.

They're celebrating the arrival of a new age.

Man 3: Wang Guoqing looks up. A crow flies with difficulty over the worn-out architecture of the city. It takes all its might to stay in the air. It may fall out of the sky any moment.

Man 1: (*lowers his head*) This city is long rot ten. Broken, disfigured! (*Coldly*) Croak, croak, croak!

Man 2: It's in the past, Guoqing. Look forward, we've still got to live.

Man 1: You know who he is?

Man 2: Yes.

Man 1: I won't let him get away.

Man 2: It's been ten years.

Man 1: I'll kill him with my own hands.

Man 2: Guoqing.

Man 1: Brother, you don't have to say no more. In the distance, the sky's blue, the water's rapid.

Man 2: I want Papa to move it, but he won't. He says he's scared.

Man 1: (*sniggers*) He's scared?

Man 3: I'm scared. I'm scared that your ma comes home and can't find me.

(*Silence. Wang Guoqing lights a cigarette, inhales and blows a smoke ring.*)

Man 1: Let's go home.

Man 2: Guoqing? Oh, right.

(*Wang Guoqing and his brother walks over to their father Wang Yiqing.*)

Man 2: Guoqing's home, pa.

Man 3: (*icily*) You're back!

Man 1: (*frostily*) I'm back.

Man 2: Pause.

Man 1: Pause.

Man 3: Pause. As if ten years have passed.

Man 1: He's aged much more than I thought. His body's parched. His back bent.

Man 3: You're all grown up, Guoqing. (*Beat*) Good that you're back –

Man 1: What's good about it?

Man 3: Guoqing, you smoke?

Man 1: In Heilongjiang in winter, if you don't smoke, you're dead.

(*As Wang Guoqing watches his father, he throws the cigarette to the floor and stamps it out. He turns around and exits.*)

(*Lights fade to blackout.*)

Character: Man 1 - Wang Guoqing, 25
Man 3 - Wang Yiqing, Guoqing's father,
in his 50s
Location: Chongqing City Hall
Time: 1979

(Lights up. Man 1 stands centre stage.)

(Night. City noises. Cacophonous)

(Man 3 appears in a corner of the stage.)

Man 3: It looks bustling at the trial. More than a hundred got sentenced at the same time. No one can remember anybody. Sitting in that dark, dense crowd, Wang Guoqing feels like an abandoned child. Wang Guoqing's kept his eyes closed and his ears keen all long, fearing that name would slip away - Ding Jianguo.

Man 1: Ding Jianguo - I open my eyes, trying hard to search from the rows of men on the stage for that man called Ding Jianguo. But they all hang their heads low. I don't know which of them is Ding Jianguo.

Man 3: Ding Jianguo, three years.

Man 1: Ding Jianguo, three years? Sentenced to three years? How could this be? One life, just three years?

Man 3: The treble horn blasts away, the sentenced paraded up, then down, row after row. Those not on stage continue to make greetings, suck on seeds, nattering and bantering, then they disperse.

Man 1: Like a dream.

Man 3: The empty hall looks dishevelled. Only two men are left. They sit far, far away. Heads down. Not talking.

Man 1: It's pouring down. The rain hits the old glass outside the hall, pounding hard.

(*The sounds of a downpour, louder and louder*)

Man 1: Wang Yiqing stands up. He walks out of the hall. The rain grows more intense. In the square outside the hall, not one person is there. The city observes the silence in the rain.

Man 3: This city just woke up, but not awake yet. Wang Guoqing stands up, but he can't move his legs. That leg doesn't feel like his.

Man 1: I stand next to him, quietly watching the rain.

Man 3: He stands next to me, not a word.

Man 1: Rain, pouring down, everything's blurry.

Man 3: Rain, pouring down, like everything's depending on it.

Man 1: A crow stands on a power line not a far away. The rain has doused its feathers. It huddles tight, totally still.

Man 3: Wang Yiqing watches that crow. It might fall any moment.

Man 1: Three years?

Man 3: Manslaughter.

Man 1: He meant it.

Man 3: Back then...

Man 1: What?

Man 3: Can't blame him completely, everyone was... mad.

Man 1: That's not a reason.

Man 3: True.

Man 1: I won't let him get away.

Man 3: What're you going to do?

Man 1: Three years.

Man 3: Three years?

Man 1: I'll wait another three years.

Man 3: Guoqing, you were young. You didn't understand. But you should know now, this is pointless.

Man 1: Yes, I was young. I didn't understand, but I know now, I'll kill him. No matter what.

Man 3: He's got what he deserved.

Man 1: (sniggers) Three years? That's enough?

Man 3: It's never enough, Guoqing.

Man 1: You work with him. You know it's him. Yet you let him off.

Man 3: Silence.

Man 1: Silence.

Man 3: Rain, pouring down, like water spilt on the ground.

Man 1: Their faces dark like stale water.

Man 3: Rain, pouring down.

Man 1: Oi, look over there.

Man 3: Wang Guoqing points at the power line by the road not far away. A crow stands on it. It's huddling tight, and it's watching him. What does it mean?

Man 3: Silence. Only the sound of rain.

Man 1: Silence. Only that crow.

(*Wang Guoqing lifts his head.*)

Man 1: He says nothing. He hunches and walks straight into the rain.

Man 3: Rain falls on my body. In no time I'm completely soaked.

Man 1: The old-man white shirt is wet through in an instant, sticking to his torso, revealing his flappy, swollen fleshiness.

Man 3: I try hard to straighten my back, my whole being drenched in rain. I seem to be crying. I don't want him to see me cry.

Man 1: I watch him slowly dissolve into the rain.

Man 3: Raining hard. All tears.

(*Wang Yiqing walks upstage and exits.*)

Man 1: Wang Guoqing lifts his head. The rain beats on his face, ice cold. He stares at the crow, as if he's also standing on the power line. Above this city, dark clouds gather. Infinite lines of rain falls from the night sky, Wang Guoqing feels his body is drifting in the rain, ascending, ascending... appraising this city from midair - it's this alien.

(*The rain hits louder and louder.*)

(*Lights fade to blackout.*)

Character: Woman 2 - wife of Wang Guoqing, in her 20s

Man 1 - Wang Guoqing, age 28

Man 3 - Wang Yiqing, Guoqing's father, in his 50s

Man 2 - Wang Guojian, Guoqing's brother, in his 30s

Woman 3 - female nurse

Location: Chongqing

Time: 1982

(Lights up. A din. Woman 3 enters.)

Man 2: It doesn't matter when. This country's always celebrating. Have a meeting, they'll celebrate for days. It's like they've never had a meeting before.

(Upstage in the light, sits Woman 2 and Man 1.)

Man 3: sits in another corner.

Woman 2: She's twenty-something. Also a rusticated youth. Now back in Chongqing, she's a worker in a textile factory. *(Forthrightly)* I'm a year younger than you. I was in Jiangxi. Where were you?

Man 1: Heilongjiang.

Woman 2: That's far.

Man 1: I chose it. The further the better.

Man 2: Guoqing went for me.

Woman 2: I've got a house. Mother just died.

Man 2: Father?

Man 1: Died more than a decade ago in the armed struggles.

Man 2: Guoqing...

Man 1: Fine.

Man 2: What?

Man 1: Fine, brother. I'll marry her.

Woman 2: We're getting married.

(*Wedding music. Two chairs appear centre stage. Wang Guoqing and his Wife sit facing each other.*)

Man 1: Thank you.

Woman 2: What for?

Man 1: For marrying me.

Woman 2: Then I've to thank you too. For marrying me.

Man 1: I'll try to be a good husband, a good father, but... Wang Guoqing looks at this wife. In the blissful happiness of her face are hints of questions.

Woman 2: What's wrong?

Man 1: I'm a man with a vendetta.

Woman 2: Vendetta?

Man 1: My mother's murder. I'll have to avenge. At all cost, even if...

Woman 2: His eyes are full of hatred. I can't help but shudder. Oh, I see.

(*The Nurse enters. She pushes a hospital bed to Wang Yiqing. He lies in it.*)

(*Wang Guoqing, his Wife and his Brother walk over. The Nurse shakes her head.*)

Man 3: You... I've got something to say to Guoqing.

(*Guoqing's Wife and Brother and the Nurse exit.*)

(*Wang Guoqing looks at his Father.*)

Man 3: Guoqing, you should smoke less.

Man 1: Right in his face, I inhale, then exhale slowly.

Man 3: Guoqing, I...

Man 1: Yeah, I'm listening.

Man 3: That afternoon, in the factory's yard, those guns that've just been handed out... His gun – I gave him. (*Beat*) The gun Ding Jianguo tried. I gave him.

Man 1: Pause.

Man 3: Pause.

Man 1: Wang Guoqing looks at his father. He can feel his head ringing.

Man 3: Guoqing?

Man 1: Wang Guoqing's clenching his fists tight. He can hear his joints pop.

Man 3: Guoqing? Guoqing!

Man 1: Wang Guoqing stares at his father.

Man 3: Guoqing...

Man 1: Wang Guoqing watches his father stiffens his body, trying to sit up. His hand extends rigidly, trying to touch his son. Wang Guoqing dodges him. He watches his father as he falls heavily back onto the bed.

Man 3: Guoqing!

Man 1: I watch him as his face gets more and more twisted.

Man 3: Guoqing, I, I...

Man 1: Wang Guoqing turns his head and stares at the monitor. His heart's beating slower and slower. Time's also slowing down.

Man 3: Guoqing!

Man 1: He struggles in the bed. But I'm not looking at him. I'm only staring at the monitor. I watch his ECG turns into a straight line.

(*Wang Yiqing convulses for a short while, then all is still. Guoqing's Brother and Wife as well as the Nurse rushes in. The Nurse bustles around.*)

Man 2: Pa! Pa! Pa!

Woman 2: Quick, call the doctor!

Woman 3: Doc, doc!

(*The Nurse exits running.*)

Woman 2: Pa, pa! Guoqing! Guoqing?

Man 1: (*goes downstage, smoking*) I saw my mother's body on the grass, blood everywhere.

(*Lights fade to blackout.*)

Character: Man 1 – Wang Guoqing, age 33
Woman 2 – wife of Wang Guoqing, in her 30s
Man 2 – Ding Jianguo, in his 40s
Man 3 – Wang Guojian, Guoqing's brother,
in his 40s
Woman 1 – waitress
Location: At home in Chonqing; a hospital in
Shanghai
Time: 1987

(Lights up. Silence. Woman 2 appears upstage.)

Woman 2: Days after days go by. This is destined to be a riotous spring. Fiery sun, desolation. This is destined to be a melancholic, hushed summer. How long has it been that everything happening in this world has nothing to do with Wang Guoqing?

(Man 1 enters.)

Man 1: I'm just plodding on.

Woman 2: Pause.

Man 1: I'm driving trucks. Always driving. I like driving. Driving on the road, I feel like I'm driving towards a defined destination. Until that day, by chance, I find out he's in Shanghai.

Woman 2: You're back.

Man 1: Yeah. *(Looks at his wife.)*

Woman 2: What's wrong?

Man 1: I found him.

Woman 2: Him? (*Surprise*) Him!

Man 1: Yes. Ding Jianguo. He's in Shanghai.

Woman 2: Guoqing, your son's doing well in his exams.

Man 1: We'll... divorce.

Woman 2: Food's ready.

Man 1: Everything's yours. Including the child. Just divorce.

Woman 2: I made the slow-cooked pork that you like

Man 1: I'm going to Shanghai.

Woman 2: Want rice?

Man 1: He's sick. In a hospital.

Woman 2: Chilies?

Man 1: I've stolen a jeep. When it's done, we'll see, maybe I won't come back.

Woman 2: They like their food sweet in Shanghai.

Man 1: If I'm alive... I'll send money back.

Woman 2: Beer? Guoqing.

Man 1: It'll be tough for you.

Woman 2: It's cold.

Man 1: I fail you, but you can't give up. This has nothing to do with you or the child.

Woman 2: ...

Man 1: Sorry.

Woman 2: I'll get you some rice.

(*Woman 2 turns around and exits.*)

Man 1: I drive the jeep to Shanghai. During the day, I find a quiet spot to kip in the car. At night, I drive. All the way I feel I'm being enveloped by darkness. Only the headlights are on, shining on all kinds of roads. Most of them are dirt tracks, dust flying everywhere. I'm like the dust churning around in the light, there's never time to settle.

(*Upstage lies Ding Jianguo in a hospital bed.*)

Man 1: I know somewhere in this world, a man called Ding Jianguo is still alive. We're like two stars. One tries to run away, one tries to hold on. We've both lost our orbits. They won't go parallel. One day, they'll clash. Only when one of them's destroyed, then the other one may get back to its own orbit.

(*Wang Guoqing walks over, with a sharp knife in his hand. He points it at Ding Jianguo.*)

Man 1: Get up.

Man 2: (*hoists himself up*) Who's that?

Man 1: You don't know me.

Man 2: Yeah.

Man 1: But I know you.

Man 2: What do you want?

Man 1: To kill you... Twenty years ago, you killed a woman.

Man 2: I didn't -

Man 1: You shut up.

Man 2: Let me explain.

Man 1: That's unnecessary.

Man 2: Who are you really?

Man 1: I'm her son.

(*Wang Guoqing stabs Ding Jianguo.*)

(*Ding falls back into the bed.*)

(*Wang cleans the knife with the bed linen, then heads downstage.*)

(*Upstage where the bed is, lights start to dim.*)

Man 1: I've played it over and over in my head how I'd kill Ding Jianguo... I pull him out of the prison, burying him alive. I intercept the prison transport, sentencing him to death in front of other criminals... and this time, I'm killing him on his sick bed.

(*Wang Guoqing blankly walks around while he mumbles.*)

Man 1: The streets of Shanghai are busy. The hospital's easy to find. At eleven forty-five, the doctors and nurses will go to the canteen for lunch. No one'll be in the ward at that time, just him. At twelve thirty, they'll be back. I only have forty five minutes. I've bought a nylon bag, rope, knife, several knifes... I've filled the jeep up, parked it outside the hospital. If he fights back, I'll kill him there and then. If he complies, I'll take him back to Chongqing, and slaughter him at mother's grave.

(*Upstage, where the hospital bed is, lights - gradually.*)

Man 1: Early that morning, I've got a seat in the restaurant opposite the hospital.

Man 1: Are you serving?

Woman 1: Breakfast or lunch?

Man 1: Lunch.

Woman 1: Bit early for that!

Man 1: Are you serving?

Woman 1: (*unwillingly*) Yeah.

(*Wang Guoqing gives the waitress his order. She takes it, then returns with a few dishes and two bottles of beers.*)

Man 1: Chewing the food, but can't taste a thing. I seem to have lost my sense of taste.

Woman 1: (*crossing her arms and looks at him*) Nutcase.

Man 1: People hover back and forth in front of me.

Man 1: (*looks at his watch*) What time is it?

Woman 1: Eleven. (*Grumbles*) Aren't you wearing a watch?

Man 1: The bill.

Woman 1: When he pays, his hand's shaking.

Man 1: She looks like at me nervously.

Woman 1: Something's wrong with him.

Man 1: Would she call the police? I go into the hospital, find a corner to squat down. I've done a recce a couple of days ago. I stash one knife on my waistline, I keep one in my hand, wrapped in newspaper. In the bag, I've got a big one. Ropes, tape, hammer... everything's ready.

Woman 1: Wang Guoqing sits on the floor. He's covered in sweat.

Man 1: How could it be this hot? It's only May.

Woman 1: His eyes never leave the door to the ward.

Man 1: It's quiet and still. No one comes in or out.

Woman 1: Eleven thirty. Wang Guoqing stands up. He wobbles, almost falls over. So, he slaps himself hard.

Man 1: A loud slap. My head rings. My whole body seems to swell up. The doctors and nurses leave with their packed lunches, chattering away.

Woman 1: His legs stride mechanically forward. A hundred metres ahead is Ding Jianguo's ward.

Man 1: Through the window, I can see someone moving.

Woman 1: Wang Guoqing checks his watch. Eleven forty.

Man 1: I freeze in the landing. I can see the drip stand with a bottle hanging.

Woman 1: Eleven forty-one.

Man 1: The ward's curtain is lifted up.

Woman 1: Wang Guoqing turns around and leaves in a hurry. He goes back to the corner.

Man 1: Fuck!

Woman 1: Eleven forty-three.

Man 1: The curtain's still moving. Fuck, it's the wind.

Woman 1: Eleven forty-four. He takes two deep breaths and knocks on his head. Eleven forty-five. He stands up and dashes over. The yard's quiet, could even hear birds chirping. The landing's a bit slippery. He almost loses his footing and falls over. He drops the nylon bag he's been carrying. It clatters. He snatches it up, throws away the paper in hand and kicks the door open.

(*Wang Guoqing dashes over to the bed upstage.*)

Woman 1: Wang Guoqing throws himself at the bed and yanks the blanket off. The bed's empty.

Man 1: My head goes numb. The bed's empty!

Woman 1: Like a caged lion, he paces around the room looking.

Man 1: Nothing, nothing, not a single soul.

Woman 1: Wang Guoqing looks at the tag on the bed. Ding Jianguo, that's right. The name on the drip, Ding Jianguo, that's right.

Man 1: Wang Guoqing walks back and forth.

Woman 1: Eleven fifty-five.

Man 1: Outside, a shadow passes, soundless.

Woman 1: Wang Guoqing dashes out of the ward. He stands in the yard, exhaling deeply.

Man 1: I've been holding my breath just now, seem to have not exhaled.

Woman 1: Wang Guoqing stands there, mumbling and fussing away.

Man 1: I can't control myself. A chill takes over my body, can't stop shaking and shivering.

Woman 1: Twelve twenty. A nurse goes into the ward.

Man 1: Wang Guoqing turns and leaves the hospital in a hurry.

(*Wang Guoqing walks rapidly away on the stage.*)

Woman 1: Midday. The sun's fierce.

Man 1: The street, full of uncaring faces.

Woman 1: Wang Guoqing feels he's drifting in the crowd.

(*Wang Guoqing stops suddenly. He stands upstage.*)

(*Man 3 enters with a phone.*)

(A clear ringtone)

(Lights upstage where the hospital bed lies. Ding Jianguo gets out of the bed and answers the call.)

Man 3: Ding Jianguo?

Man 2: Yes.

Man 3: I'm Wang Guojian.

Man 2: Wang Guojian?

Man 3: Wang Yiqing's son. Elder son.

Man 2: Hi.

Man 3: You're in Shanghai?

Man 2: ...

Man 3: My brother went to Shanghai.

Man 2: ...

Man 3: He knows which hospital you're in. He's coming to find you.

Man 2: ...

Man 3: He's been looking for you... You... should lie low.

(*Wang Guojian hangs up.*)

(*The sound of a phone hanging up, exaggerated. Ding Jianguo hangs up, looking haunted and lost, exits in a run.*)

Man 1: Brother?! Bro!

(*Wang Guojian looks at his brother, emotionless.*)

Man 1: Why?

(*The knife Wang Guoqing is holding falls on the ground.*)

Man 2: Croak, croak, croak!

Man 1: A crow croaks as it flies. It's flying really fast.

Man 2: It quickly disappears into the Shanghai night.

Man 1: Shanghai in June 1987 can actually be this cold.

(*Lights fade to blackout.*)

Character: Man 1 - Wang Guoqing, age 46
Man 2 - Ding Liming, son of Ding
Jianguo and a judge in Shanghai,
about 30 years old
Man 3
Woman 1
Woman 2
Woman 3
Location: The Bund, Shanghai
Time: 2000

(*Lights up*)

(*The light and sound of fireworks*)

(*Man 3, Woman 1, Woman 2 and Woman 3 stroll on the stage.*)

(*Ding Liming walks between them. A smile on his face*)

(*Wang Guoqing appears in a corner of the stage, watching Ding.*)

Man 2: The last night of Y2K. Millennium night! Once every thousand years. Shanghai, the Bund, people everywhere.

Man 1: Fireworks explode in the sky, vanishing in a blink. Flickers light the faces of the crowd looking up. The city at night is moaning and groaning as if it's about to come.

Man 2: Amidst in the crowd, so packed that nothing's standing straight, Wang Guoqing watches people's cheers and their inexplicable excitement. Buffered by the crowd, he's eyes only for one person.

Man 1: Buffered by the crowd, my eyes never leave him. His face, full of hope, future, determination.

Man 2: Ding Liming cuts through the crowd, like a minnow in its elements. To be in Shanghai, to be a judge, that's his life's dream.

Man 1: A man can disappear for ten years with out a trace. But there's always some signs.

(*Wang Guoqing circles Ding Liming, appraising him.*)

Man 1: After more than a decade, I haven't been able to find Ding Jianguo, but I found his son, Ding Liming.

Man 2: A judge.

Man 1: A minnow.

Man 2: Minnow?

Man 1: A small fish that swims fast. They've got one that leads, whether right or wrong, the shoal follows. I'll give you a term. It's also for me.

Man 2: A term?

Man 1: Yes. When my mother died, I was thir teen. So, you'll have thirteen years.

Man 2: Thirteen years?

Man 1: Thirteen years. If after thirteen years, you're still a good person, I'll let you off.

Man 2: Good? (*Laughs*) What's good?

Man 1: We'll use the standard that applies to most people - the law.

Man 2: The law?

Man 1: In the next thirteen years, if you stay on the right side of the law, I'll let you off.

Man 2: You haven't got the power.

Man 1: Power? (*Laughs*) Your father gave it to me.

Man 2: My father?

Man 1: His name's Ding Jianguo.

Man 2: Ding Jianguo, that man I call father, is far away in the horizon, drifting.

(*Man 3, Woman 1, Woman 2 and Woman 3 exit.*)

Man 2: Far away, that man. He looks at people funny. He's in the crowd, but has nothing to do with the people.

Man 1: Everyone else doesn't seem to exist. Only you and me. Man to man.

Man 2: The fireworks are done. The crowd creeps along in the dark. So many people. Who's good? Who's bad?

Man 1: Maggots in a pit of shit.

Man 2: The city, panting.

Man 1: Lights dim.

Man 2: Darkness, is just a placebo. It masks the issue, but it can't stop the pain.

(*Wang Guoqing and Ding Liming stare at each other.*)

Man 1: What're they cheering about?

Man 2: Into the new millennium, we've long been broken.

(*Lights fade to blackout.*)

Character: Man 1 - Ding Guoqing, age 54

Man 2 - Ding Liming

Man 3 - husband of Ding's cousin

Woman 1 - Ding's wife

Woman 2 - Ding's cousin

Woman 3 - Ding's daughter, Ding's lover

Location: Shanghai, Beijing

Time: 2008

(Lights up)

(Wang Guoqing is wearing a mackintosh, standing silently. He's shivering a little, his body shudders.)

(Others stand at a corner of the stage, watching him. They're in a stand off.)

Man 3: Silence!

Man 2: Boom, boom, boom...

Woman 1: Silence!

Man 2: Boom, boom, boom...

Woman 2: Silence!

Man 2: Boom, boom, boom...

Woman 1: Silence!

Man 2: Boom, boom, boom! So quiet that you can hear the heart beats.

Man 3: Standing in front of the notice board, Wang Guoqing can't find a trace of his protest letter posted a week ago

(*Wang Guoqing shouts with all his might. He huddles and squats. But he can't make a sound.*)

Man 3: Silence!

Woman 1: Silence!

Woman 2: Silence!

Woman 3: Silence!

Man 2: Silence! No one cares, no one!

Man 3: Vanished.

Woman 1: Silenced.

Woman 2: Gone.

Woman 3: Unheard.

Man 2: ...

Man 3: It's happened, but like nothing's happened.

Man 2: Unexpected, but within expectation.

Man 3: Wang Guoqing knew it'd be so.

Man 2: He's just one in the shoal of minnow. He's never the lead one.

(*Wang Guoqing stands up slowly.*)

Man 1: I feel I'm a crow standing on a power line. I cry with my life, but no one hears me.

(*The crow opens its beak and croaks.*)

Man 2: Croak, croak, croak!

(*More and more sounds from the city: people, cars, noisy and indistinct*)

(*The sound gets louder and louder. A wall of noise that drowns the crow's croak.*)

(*It quiets down. Silence*)

(*The crow's beak is still open, but no sound comes out.*)

Man 2: ...

Man 3: Silence!

Woman 1: Silence!

Woman 2: Silence!

Woman 3: Silence!

Man 1: Such a big city, like it's dead. I can only hear my heartbeat. It's very rhythmic, the war drums that push me to march forward.

(*Distant thunder*)

Man 3: Thunder, rolling closer from the distance.

Woman 3: The city, antsy.

Woman 1: The air, stifling.

Man 1: I'm walking on the street, sweat dripping non-stop. People around seem blurry, phantom-like, silently gliding past me. I keep on walking, determination powers my body.

(*Wang Guoqing walks rapidly.*)

Woman 2: I've got someone inside.

Man 1: I know who he is. I start to run, like I'm inexhaustible.

Woman 2: I've got someone above me.

Man 1: I know who he is.

Woman 2: You can't win.

Man 1: This is just the beginning. I'm running.

Woman 2: Let it go. What's the point? Ain't no smoke without a fire.

Man 1: I'll find the fire. Why I'm dealing with you? I'm waiting for him to move.

Woman 2: Him? Who?

Woman 3: The crow flies.

Man 3: It's raining.

Man 1: He makes a move. He's not a good person. That's enough. I've got my warrant. It's my turn.

Woman 3: The crow flies away.

Man 1: I'm your stealthy shadow of the night. But when I raise the knife, it glimmers, so I lose my shadow.

Woman 3: It's raining. The peach blossoms have bloomed.

Man 1: I bought four cars. Changed different drivers. To follow him.

Man 3: Boss?

Man 1: Follow him.

Man 2: Missus, I'm back.

Woman 1: Finished for the day? Must be tired.

Man 2: Yeah, never ending cases.

Woman 2: Boss?

Man 1: Follow him... This is not his home?

Woman 2: Boss?

Man 1: You drive back first.

Woman 2: What about you?

Man 1: I'll make my own way.

Man 2: Wifey, I'm back.

Woman 3: Who's your wife? I'm like a cat on a hot tin roof, took you so long. Come in, quick.

Man 2: I know you can't wait.

Man 1: I stoop by the door, watching my watch, watching my second hand move, then minute, then hour. Two hours. Son of a bitch. He's got some stamina.

Man 3: Boss?

Man 1: Same as before.

Man 2: Missus, you been to our daughter's parents meeting?

Woman 1: Yeah, you do remember.

Man 2: Busy.

Woman 1: It's just you.

Man 2: I won't be back tomorrow night.

Woman 1: Again?

Man 2: Got a case.

Woman 2: Boss, keep watching him?

Man 1: Yeah.

Man 2: Darling, I'm back.

Woman 3: Why're you so late?

Man 2: Got to go to my daughter's parents meeting.

Woman 3: You?

Man 2: Fine, won't talk about that.

Woman 3: Won't let you go tonight.

Man 2: Fine, I won't leave.

(*Wang Guoqing goes to the centre of the stage and hesitates for a long time. Then he knocks.*)

(*Ding Liming's mistress opens the door.*)

Woman 3: What?

Man 1: Oh, I'm from the courier.

Woman 3: (eyes Wang up and down) Courier?

Man 1: This is Flat 603, right?

Woman 3: No, this is 1603.

Man 1: I'm sorry, my mistake.

(*Ding's mistress shuts the door.*)

Man 2: Who's that?

Woman 3: Delivery. Got the wrong flat.

Man 1: (*calls on his phone*) Hi... I want to report Judge Ding Liming...

(*Wang Guoqing hangs up*)

Man 3: He's got three properties, each worth more than ten million. His wife doesn't work. He's also kept a mistress...

Man 1: None of these is fatal... So, I went to Beijing.

(*The crow opens its beak, but it's making no sound.*)

Man 2: ...

Man 3: Silence!

Woman 1: Silence!

Woman 2: Silence!

Woman 3: Silence!

(*The cast take off Wang Guoqing's ragged old clothes and dress him in a suit, leather shoes and mackintosh. With a leather bag in his hand, Wang looks fresh and spirited.)*

Man 1: I'm not a visitor and I'm not here with a petition.

Woman 1: State Bureau for Letters and Calls.

Man 3: Name: Wang Guoqing.

Woman 2: Central Political and Legal Commission.

Man 3: Gender: Male.

Woman 1: Supreme People's Court.

Man 3: Age: Fifty six.

Woman 2: Tiananmen Square.

Man 3: Ethnicity: Han.

Man 1: I want to report Judge Ding Liming!

Man 2: Beijing's winter. The wind cuts your face like a knife.

Man 1: The wind pulls my hair, howling with abandonment all around. The gigantic Tiananmen Square, empty. Only the distinct neon flickering restlessly. A crow died from the cold lies stiffly on the concrete. Its claws clenched, as if trying to clutch onto something. But there's only the cold wind.

Woman 1: A street cleaner walks past, she sweeps the dead crow into her pan.

Man 1: I'm being swept into the pan by that woman, then tipped into the bin. My stiff body hits the bin with a thud.

Woman 1: The thud instantly disappears into the cold wind, without a trace.

Woman 3: I once roamed the sky, always brooding.

Woman 2: A policeman walks over.

Man 3: Oi, what're you doing?

Man 1: Nothing.

Man 3: What're you doing here?

Man 1: Me?

Man 3: ID.

(*Wang Guoqing digs out his ID, stunned, then passes it onto the Policeman. He looks at it.*)

Man 3: Name.

Man 1: Wang Guoqing.

Man 3: Gender.

Man 1: Male.

Man 3: Age.

Man 1: Fifty six.

Man 3: What's in your bag?

Man 1: Papers.

Man 3: Open it.

(*The Policeman looks into Wang's briefcase, hands the ID back, then leaves.*)

Man 3: Move, move along!

Man 1: Right.

Woman 2: A middle-aged man walks over.

Man 2: Here to watch the flag raising? Another six hours to go.

Man 1: No.

Man 2: No? Then I suggest you leave.

Man 1: ...

Man 2: Would you?

Man 1: I'll go now.

Man 2: Get smarter, this is not somewhere you can hang around.

Man 1: I really want to beat the drum and make my petition now. But, where's my drum?

(*In the distance, intense drumbeats, getting louder.*)

(*Lights fade to blackout.*)

Character: Man 1 - Wang Guoqing, age 56
               Man 2 - Ding Liming, in his 40s
               Man 3 - dancer in the square
               Woman 3 - dancer in the square
               Woman 1 - girl
               Woman 2
Location: Shanghai
Time: 2010

(Lights up)

(A man and a woman sit at the opposite ends of the stage. They wear the same outfit: floral shirt, white trousers, black leather shoes.)

(They look at each other.)

Man 3: Dusk. The sun hasn't set yet. In a street corner park sits a man and a woman. They're both old, but it's impossible to tell their age. They're dressed immaculately.

(The Woman eventually stands up. She tries to twist from her waist, a few dance steps. Becoming a bit self-conscious, she stops.)

Man 3: The man looks at her. He asks quietly, 'New here?'

Woman 3: No. You?

Man 3: No.

Woman 3: Haven't seen you before.

Man 3: Me neither.

Woman 3: You know how to dance?

Man 3: No.

Woman 3: Me neither.

Man 3: No, you're doing great.

Woman 3: It's embarrassing.

Man 3: Same here.

Woman 3: The woman looks at the man. She can't verbalise it. Silence.

Man 3: Silence.

Woman 3: He looks at his watch.

(*Man 3 looks at his watch.*)

Man 3: She runs her hand through her neatly done hair and turns her head away.

Woman 3: The sky's stained red in the west. Rays of sun still struggling between the curtain walls of skyscrapers, flashing dazzles of gold. He's looking at me?

Man 3: The man's looking at the woman.

Woman 3: The woman turns her head. He's looking at me. (*Smiles*) We're early.

Man 3: It's all right.

Woman 3: Yes, it's all right.

(*Two couples enter. They also wear the same outfit.*)

(*The Man and the Woman both immediately become much more at ease.*)

(*One of the men is carrying a boombox. He presses a button, loud, popular music bursts forth. Following the music, the three couples start to dance. The steps are simple and crude. The dance look boring and monotonous, but the dancers are revelling in the process.*)

(*One of the men gradually dances out of the crowd. He stops, watching them ponderously. He takes off his floral shirt. He is Wang Guoqing.*)

Man 1: Wang Guoqing watches these dancers in the square. They were once section heads, division directors, bureau chiefs. Blue collar, white collar, gold collar. Professors, teachers, clerks! But now, they're all dancers in the square.

(*One of the women gradually dances out of the crowd. She stops, watching them ponderously. She takes off her floral shirt. She is the Girl.*)

Man 1: A girl strides into this street corner. She starts yelling at the dancers angrily.

Woman 1: (*with her hands on her waist*) Stop dancing. Stop the racket.

Man 1: The music and the dancing continue. No one pays any attention.

Woman 1: (*with her hands on her waist*) Haven't you got anything in there? You're already this old!

Man 1: The music and the dancing continue. No one pays any attention.

Woman 1: (*with her hands on her waist*) You know this is public nuisance, eh? I'm going to sue you. You've got family, kids. Don't you realise other people still need to live? Don't you understand reason? Aren't you human? You've already lived so long, how come you're still so selfish. Are you all animals? I'm talking about you. I'm having a go at you! God, what's going on? Are you all idiots? Idiots! Idiots!

(*One of the men walks to the boombox. He moves a dial, the music becomes louder.*)

Man 1: The girl watches them.

(*The Girls watches this group. She gradually calms down. Then slowly puts on the floral shirt and join in the dance again.*)

Man 1: Wang Guo watches these people. He's a bit frightened. He longs to be them, but is also scared of becoming them.

(*Music fades out. The dancers take off their floral shirts. They walk around the stage, Wang Guoqing weaves in and out.*)

Man 1: Wang Guoqing walks along on the streets. He feels an eagle is circling over his head. So he buys a pair of glasses with a video camera and starts to make plans. One year, two, three. He's not rushed. To catch a fox, you'll have to be craftier. This is a war between two men. He's on relying on the crowd, but he can use them.

(*Three men wobble drunkenly across the stage.*)

Man 3: Liming, it's fine. Lawyer Zhang'll fork the bill. The girls're great. Take your pick!

Man 2: That lad, he's learning. That case ain't so simple! Is it safe here?

Man 1: Don't worry. Old haunt.

Man 2: (*slurring*) Thing goes tits up... got you...

Man 1: They sell. We buy. Everyone's willing. Fair trade. How can it go tits up?

Man 3: Tips, you just give them. Lawyer Zhang'll get them back for you.

Man 2: That lad, getting generous...

(*Three women enter, dressed as nurse, police and student. They walk seductively in front of the men. They ogle lecherously.*)

Man 1: The student ain't bad, I'll take her.

Man 2: You old fart lusting after young things. Don't flag.

Man 1: Liming, don't you worry. I've still got it.

Man 3: Liming, you pick. I'm happy with either the nurse or the copper.

Man 2: I see female copper everyday, they don't do it for me. I'll have the nurse.

(*Everyone exits except Wang Guoqing.*)

Man 1: Karaoke two hours. Dinner three hours. Private room four hours.

(*Ding Liming enters. He looks at Wang Guoqing from a distance. Wang turns to watch him. They seem to recognise each other. Ding walks toward Wang and walks on past him. Wang turns to watch Ding exit.*)

Man 1: This year, I've been following him. We've come face to face many times. I thought he saw me, but each time, we just walked past each other.

(*The light on Wang Guoqing dims.*)

Character: Man 1 – Wang Guoqing, age 58
Man 2 – Ding Liming, in his 40s
Man 3
Woman 1
Woman 2
Woman 3
Location: A funeral home in Shanghai
Time: 2012

(Lights up)

(Funeral music. In the centre of the stage, Man 3 and three women are standing with the back to the audience. They are dressed in black from head to toe.)

(Downstage, Ding Liming is standing solemnly with his arms by his side. Wang Guoqing enters.)

Man 1: Midday. The sun's glorious, but inside the funeral home death prevails. Other than funereal music, the only signs of life are the occasionally bursts of desperate wailing. I spent fifty kuai on a wreath and walks into the memorial hall for this deceased. I don't know who he is, but I know his son-in-law is called Ding Liming, the judge that I've followed for twelve years.

(*Wang Guoqing goes up to take Ding Liming's hand.*)

Man 1: My condolences.

Man 2: Thank you.

Man 1: He takes my hand, a firm grasp. Warm. His eyes are full of gratitude. I look right at him, and he does the same. His cheek rosy, a gentile face. Time's treated him well. But in the corners of his eyes are hints of suspicion and sly.

Man 2: This man looks a bit familiar. Where've I seen him?

Man 1: I've to go. I can't make his suspicious. Take care.

(*Wang Guoqing goes.*)

Man 2: Thank you.

Man 1: He doesn't know me, but I know him. I stand at the back of the crowd, watching him quietly. Like the eagle beyond the cloud, silently watching the crows on the trees. For half an hour, that's how I watch him. It's a wonderful feeling.

Man 2: Quiet.

Man 1: Only funereal music moves before my eyes.

Man 2: I hate funeral homes. They make everything meaningless.

Man 1: Funeral homes are great places. They make you look beyond life and death.

Man 2: Positions, status, women, money, they're smoke and mirrors.

Man 1: I've followed him for so long. I've collected so much evidence. Each one's solid, but none of them can pull him off the pedestal.

Man 2: You only live once, might as well have some fun.

Man 1: Doesn't matter. I'll wait. I know he can't control it down there.

Man 2: They all look really sad.

Man 1: The man in the portrait smiles. A bit creepy.

Man 2: Their faces drawn. Their eyes tearful. For him? Or for themselves? Pause.

Man 1: Pause.

(*Ding Liming turns around to look at Wang Guoqing abruptly. They look at each other. Wang Guoqing forces out a hint of a smile. The crowd disperses.*)

Man 1: (*goes forward*) Take care.

Man 2: Thank you.

Man 1: Goodbye.

Man 2: Goodbye.

(*Ding Liming watches Wang Guoqing exits. Funereal music fades out.*)

(*Lights fade to blackout.*)

Character: Man 1 – Wang Guoqing, age 60
Man 2 – Ding Liming, in his 40s
Woman 2 – prostitute
Man 3 – security, Ding Jianguo
Location: A private members club in Shanghai
Time: 2014

(*Darkness. A man is panting hard.*)

Man 3: Darkness! Can't see anything.

Man 2: Darkness! Can feel everything. Banging, one after another. Unstoppable, insane banging. Each one takes this man closer to a more pleasurable apogee.

Man 3: Darkness! Can't see anything.

Man 2: Darkness! I bump it away time after time. I can see the whole world.

Man 3: Darkness! Oppresses everything.

Man 2: Darkness! Allows everything to expand rapidly. Growing bigger. Growing stronger. The apogee of pleasure. I become fireworks.

Man 3: The fireworks explode in the night sky, dazzling.

Man 2: I light up the night sky.

Man 3: Darkness, gone.

Man 2: I see my twisted, deformed face.

(*Lights up gradually. Ding Liming and the nurse fasten their clothes.*)

Man 3: Man is a strange animal. Spend so much time in the chase, then just in a few seconds, they fall from the sky back to earth.

Man 2: I feel I'm –

Woman 2: A pig.

Man 2: ...?

Woman 2: Man, you've really got it.

Man 2: Really?

Woman 2: Someone almost couldn't handle it.

Man 2: So is it got it or can't handle it?

Woman 2: Shameless. You've got it, someone can't handle it.

Man 2: I'll come to you next time.

Woman 2: Man, you're mean, turn around and know no one.

Man 2: I just need to know you.

(*Wang Guoqing enters wearing glasses. He goes close to Ding Liming and the nurse, circling them, watching.*)

Man 1: Right. Here. Slower.

Man 3: What did you drop?

Man 1: A briefcase.

Man 3: You can call the police.

Man 1: You're funny. I was here for the ladies, and you let me call the police?

Man 3: You really, did you have too much fun... (*Laughs*) You should be more careful next time.

Man 1: Just take it back, here.

(*Wang Guoqing circles Ding Liming and the nurse. Ding is holding her hand.*)

Man 1: Right, this part, slower. Let me see. Yes, this is the man. I've seen him. I've still got the bag in my hand then.

Man 3: You've watched lots of times.

Man 1: Fine, looks like it's gone.

Man 3: Why did you bring a bag for the ladies? All you need is a pouch.

Man 1: Pouch?

Man 3: (*Laughs*) You know.

Man 1: Oooh, you're bad.

Man 3: We're not as bad as you. We're the security, we can only watch the tapes. Unlike you, you don't even need to watch. Just do it.

(*Ding Liming and the nurse exit.*)

(*Wang Guoqing points in the direction where Ding has gone. He turns around to look at Man 3.*)

Man 1: You've got to hit it where it hurts.

Man 3: He's my son.

Man 1: I don't care where you're hiding. He's where it hurts.

(*Ding Jianguo exits.*)

(*Wang Guoqing takes his glasses off and looks at it*)

Man 1: Glasses that shoot video. What a fucking great invention. Now, it's my turn.

(*Lights fade to blackout.*)

Character: Man 1 - Wang Guoqing, age 60
               Man 2 - Ding Jianguo, age 70
               Man 3
               Woman 1
               Woman 2
               Woman 3
Location: Online
Time: 2014

(*Lights up. Three men and three women appear on stage.*)

(*Sounds of typing and the different noises the internet makes.*)

Man 3: Internet, what a great place!

Woman 1: Behind every symbol's the shape of men.

Woman 2: Randomly pick a nickname, you can rant about anyone. After your rant, nobody knows who you are.

Woman 3: Those with a name ends in your month, you can bite and tear as you like. As long as he's flesh and blood, you'll find somewhere to snap your jaws on.

Woman 1: You're a rabid dog lurking in the dark, ready to pounce. You're never worried because the shouts would bring in a crowd. People like watching dogs bite men, as long as they stay clear of the action.

Woman 2: They'd love to watch a man bite a dog, but not many are willing to bear their teeth at a dog. Otherwise, they'd get an even bigger crowd.

Woman 3: In conclusion: the man get mauled all over, the dog has its day, barking away.

Woman 1: As long as it's someone else being bitten, no one'd care whether it's a dog - or a pig - that's doing the pouncing.

Woman 2: They lurk in the dark, their teeth sharpened, ready to dash out, to bite.

Woman 3: Bite, bite furiously.

Woman 1: Hounding people with labels, acting like pigs and dogs. Bite.

Man 3: She's a mistress.

Woman 1: Bite.

Woman 2: She's dressed like that.

Woman 3: Bite.

Man 2: He's a druggie.

Woman 1: Bite.

Man 3: He's moved up.

Woman 1: Bite.

Woman 2: His wage?

Woman 3: Bite.

Man 2: He's at a restaurant?

Woman 1: Bite.

Man 3: He's bought a house.

Woman 1: Bite.

Woman 2: He's been to the toilet twice in the morning.

Woman 3: Bite.

Man 2: He's actually human.

Woman 1: Bite.

Man 3: Who's he?

Woman 1: Bite.

Woman 2: Who's he?

Woman 3: Tear him apart.

Man 2: Who's he?

Woman 1: Tear whoever he's apart.

Woman 1: Bite.

Man 3: Bite.

Woman 1: Bite.

Woman 2: Bite.

Woman 3: Bite.

Man 2: Bite.

Woman 1: Bite.

All: Bite.

Man 1: I register an account, pick a name without much thought. Then I upload the edited video online and ask a few friends to repost. Then, the biting begins.

(Sounds of dogs barking and fighting, in crescendo)

Man 1: Half an hour.

Woman 1: Wang Guoqing sits in front of the computer. He watches the number of reposts shoot up.

Man 2: One hour.

Woman 2: We can smell blood.

Man 3: Two hours.

Woman 3: Dog bites dog, dog bites man, man bites dog, man bites man...

Man 2: Judge visits hooker. Repost.

Woman 1: Judge pays for sex. Repost.

Man 3: Scandal. Repost.

Woman 2: Exciting. Repost.

Woman 3: Lordy. Repost.

Man 2: Fab. Repost.

Woman 1: Feck. Repost.

Man 3: Repost.

Woman 2: Repost.

Woman 3: Repost.

Man 2: Scum.

Woman 1: Criminal.

Man 3: Kill him.

Woman 2: Kill him.

Woman 3: Kill him.

Man 1: They're angrier than me.

Woman 1: Dogs, always seem angrier than men.

Man 2: Three hours later.

Man 3: Wang Guoqing deletes the video, deletes the account.

Woman 1: The storm's broken.

Man 2: Five hours later.

Woman 2: Viewers, we've just received the news. A video of a judge visiting prostitutes has been leaked online...

Man 2: Seven hours later.

Woman 3: The video of Judge Ding Liming in the act with a prostitute has gone viral...

Man 2: The next day.

Woman 1: Are you Wang Guoqing?

Man 2: The municipal's Discipline Commission and High Court are investigating the incident of five judges including Ding Liming visiting prostitutes...

Woman 2: Aren't you afraid of revenge?

Man 2: The Municipal Party Committee announce the verdict for the judge prostitution case...

Woman 3: Why are you exacting revenge?

Man 3: The analysis to the details of the judge prostitution case...

Woman 1: How did you get first hand information?

Man 2: The whole story of the judge prostitution case...

Man 3: One week later, these'll all be text symbols on the internet. No one'll remember.

Woman 1: People get on with their lives.

Woman 2: Dogs keep their jaws open wide.

Woman 3: Bite.

Man 3: Bite.

Woman 1: Bite.

Woman 2: Bite.

(*A phone rings. Man 2 is dialing. Wang Guoqing picks up his mobile.*)

Man 1: Hi! Hello! Hello?

Man 2: I am Ding Jianguo. I am in Hong Kong. Come. I will be waiting for you!

Woman 1: The rain grows more and more intense.

Woman 2: Lights dim.

(*The sound of rain*)

(*Lights fade to blackout.*)

Character: Man 1 - Wang Guoqing, age 60

Man 2 - Ding Jianguo, age 70

Man 3

Woman 1

Woman 2

Woman 3

Location: Hong Kong

Time: 2014

(Lights up)

(The sound of rain getting louder)

(Man 3, Woman 1, Woman 2 and Woman 3 are all wearing raincoats, wrapped tight. They stand silently in the centre of the stage.)

Woman 1: Because of the sun, I wrestle out from the sea. I dance happily in the air, rising steadily. The temperature gets lower, I bump into you.

Woman 2: There's no more you. Or me.

Woman 3: I keep rising. More and more water droplets. Tiny droplets. We keep rising.

Woman 1: We bump into each other. We gather.

Woman 2: That's me. I'm the cloud, building up in the night sky.

Woman 3: Getting thicker.

Woman 1: Getting colder.

Woman 2: Raindrops come together in the cloud.

Woman 3: I come together in your body.

Woman 2: I can't hold you.

Woman 1: I wrestle out of the cloud, shouting, crying, happily rush to the ground.

Woman 2: We run towards the ground together.

Woman 3: Sliding past skyscrapers, treetops, towards the ground.

Woman 1: The rain falling ceaselessly!

Woman 2: Down, down!

Woman 3: Hitting the ground, hitting on bodies. Dispersed.

Woman 2: Wang Guoqing listens to the rain outside. Dense. Knocking on his heart.

Man 1: I'm staring at the clock on the wall. Watching the second hand goes forward bit by bit. But the minute hand seems to be static. Wang Guoqing looks at his phone. Three forty-seven a.m.

Woman 3: From beyond the window comes a low and deep singing. Barely audible, distant, rolling over like the thunder, and rolling away in the city's night sky.

Woman 2: The grassland after the rainy season, the stampeding herd.

(*Man 3 hums a song - a march.*)

Man 3: Hum...!

Woman 3: Wang Guoqing sits up. Darkness envelopes him. He can hear blood flowing, through his face, his chest, even to the tip of his hair.

(*Wang Guoqing suddenly appears in the light. He's standing and he's naked.*)

Woman 1: Lightning glows without reason. Outside, the dark night opens its mouth, swallowing everything.

Man 1: I crawl up from the bed. My feet touch the ground, as if stepping on spring.

Woman 2: Wang Guoqing hobbles to the window.

Woman 3: Outside, pitch black. Occasional lightning in the distance, illuminating the thick clouds, far, far away.

Man 3: Hum...!

Man 3: Wang Guoqing walks to the bathroom. The floor's moist. His feet curl. The floor's cold.

Woman 2: He turns on the light. It actually works.

Woman 1: At the first moment of light, he can't help but sway, not quite steady on his feet, can't see clearly.

Woman 3: Wang Guoqing turns the tap, splashing water onto his face, drinking a few gulps in the process.

Woman 2: The water's cool. He feels much more awake.

Woman 1: The cold water travels down the esophagus

into his stomach, pulling him from midair back to the ground.

Woman 2: He turns on the shower. Water gushes out.

Man 1: Water hits my body. I can't help but shudder.

Man 3: Hong Kong, July 2014. A hotel in Central. Eleven minutes past four in the morning. Cold water hits Wang Guoqing's body. He shudders violently.

Woman 1: Pants... t-shirt... trousers... shirt... suit... socks... tie... leather shoes... watch...

Woman 2: Four thirty-two a.m.

Woman 1: Wang Guoqing is dressed.

Woman 2: He checks his bag once more.

Woman 3: Hammer... kitchen knife... chopper... dagger... nylon bag... rope... balaclava... entry permit... train ticket... wallet...

Woman 2: He pulls out an RMB note. The person on it is laughing.

Man 3: Ha ha ha!

Woman 2: Door card... door... No one's in the lift.

Woman 1: Four forty-one.

Woman 3: Ding...

Woman 2: The receptionist looks up, sleepy.

Man 1: Hi.

Woman 1: Going out?

Man 1: Yeah.

Woman 1: Take care.

Man 1: Bye.

Man 3: The lobby's empty. Wang Guoqing pushes the glass door hard.

Woman 2: The wind blows his tie up, onto his face.

Woman 3: The rain falls ruthlessly on him.

Man 1: Fuck, forgot the brollie.

Man 3: You never needed one.

Man 1: Wang Guoqing heads into the rain. The rain follows his hair, cheek, neck, into this body.

(*Wang Guoqing walks rapidly. Man 3, Woman 1, Woman 2 and Woman 3 put on rain hats. They follow him, encircling him, even pulling him back. He moves forward with difficulty.*)

Woman 1: Wang Guoqing walks in the rain.

Woman 2: Wang Guoqing walks on the streets of Central.

Woman 3: Wang Guoqing walks amidst the crowd.

Woman 1: Rain, falling harder, hitting the ground, the people, wildly.

Woman 2: The streets are full of people, dense and packed.

Woman 3: They're singing.

Man 3: Hum...

Woman 1: People are sitting quietly.

Woman 2: People are sitting quietly on the street.

Woman 3: People are sitting quietly in the rain.

Man 3: Hum...

Woman 1: Wang Guoqing walks through the crowd.

Woman 2: He steps onto their clothes.

Woman 3: No one moves.

Woman 1: His bag bumps into people.

Woman 2: No one moves.

Woman 3: He kicks someone hard. He falls, on someone.

(*Wang Guoqing falls.*)

Woman 1: No one moves.

Man 3: Hum...

Man 1: Sorry.

Woman 2: No one moves.

Woman 3: Wang Guoqing climbs up from the crowd.

(*Wang Guoqing climbs up.*)

Woman 1: People are looking ahead. In the distance, the black building squats there like the devil. It's been plastered with all kinds of slogans. It looks ridiculous. Wang Guoqing seems to have seen it somewhere before.

Woman 2: Wang Guoqing moves forward in the crowd with difficulty.

Woman 3: People are sitting upright, looking right into the distance.

Man 3: Hum...

Woman 1: The rain falls densely on Wang Guoqing's face.

Woman 2: He seems to be floating in the rain.

Woman 3: Being washed to a distant place.

Man 3: Hum...

Woman 1: Wang Guoqing gets out of the crowd with difficulty.

Woman 2: The streets are deserted.

Woman 3: Four fifty-nine a.m.

Man 3: Amidst the sound of the rain, Wang Guoqing can hear his own footsteps. Very rapid.

(*Wang Guoqing shakes off everyone else and starts to run. Man 3, Woman 1, Woman 2 and Woman 3 walk slowly to the end of the stage.*)

(*Wang Guoqing runs with all his might.*)

Woman 1: Embankment.

Woman 2: Standing there icily.

Woman 3: The sea.

Woman 1: Rolling as if it's boiling.

Woman 2: Blackness, rolling.

Woman 3: Spitting white foam. Miserable.

Man 3: Five a.m. In the wind and rain, Wang Guoqing runs through the streets of Hong Kong.

Woman 1: The city's enormous. Standing there hushed.

Woman 2: The clouds shroud the skyscrapers. Everything becomes illusionary.

Woman 3: Rain, wind, wave, the distant song.

Man 3: Hum...

(*Ding Jianguo suddenly appears in the light. He's wearing a suit, standing silently. Wang Guoqing stops in front of him.*)

Woman 3: Rain keep washing down.

(*Sound of a downpours*)

Man 3: They eye each other wordlessly.

Man 1: The rain rolls down his face with abandonment. He squints, looking at me.

Man 2: The rain hits his face. His eyes widen, looking at me.

Man 1: His lips tightly pursed. I can't see his gaze. He's so old!

Woman 3: Rain, wind, wave, the distant song.

Woman 1: Sh!

Woman 2: Silence.

Woman 3: Wang Guoqing can hear his heartbeat.

Man 2: I am Ding Jianguo.

Man 3: Wang Guoqing's hand clenches onto the bag.

Woman 1: Sky, intensely blue.

Man 2: I want to forget... that time...

Woman 2: Still.

Man 2: People lost their reason. Everyone. I was just one of them.

Woman 3: The sun's venomous.

Man 2: I didn't know what I was doing, and... I killed your mother.

Man 3: Crows circle in the sky.

Man 2: I was a young man. I believed - blindly believed. I believed the power of the masses. So many people, got to be right. No one was thinking. Thinking was laughable, useless. Everyone's doing that, it's got to be right. We become crazed, cruel, savage...

Woman 1: The woman's face, pallid.

Man 2: Sorry. I know you've been looking for me. Your father, your brother, your wife, your son... I know you - everything about you.

Woman 2: Blood gushes from her chest, relentless, onto the patch of grass.

Man 2: From Chongqing to Shanghai, from Shanghai to Beijing.

Woman 3: Grass, intensely green.

Man 2: You destroyed my son.

Man 1: He deserves it.

Man 3: They eye each other wordlessly.

(*Ding Jianguo pulls out a gun, pointing straight at Wang Guoqing. Wang takes a step back.*)

Woman 1: Rain, falling harder.

Man 2: I've been running away. You never let go.

Woman 2: Wind, cuts the face, painful.

Man 2: It's not his fault. Ding Liming, my son.

Woman 3: The sea crashes into the embankment, breaking down thunderously.

Woman 1: Can't tell between the sea and the rain.

(*Ding Jianguo turns the gun around slowly.*)

Man 2: Hey, know you wouldn't have a gun. Here.

(*Wang Guoqing watches Ding Jianguo. He takes the gun slowly and points it at Ding.*)

Man 2: Sorry.

Woman 1: A gun is this heavy.

Man 2: I'm seventy this year. I've run for forty odd years. It's time to end.

Woman 2: Rain falls on Wang Guoqing's hands, splashing, dissipating into the wind.

Man 2: Should've ended long ago.

Man 1: Rain falls on his face. He's been squinting. Rain thrashes on his face, like tears.

Man 2: Rain courses down his grizzled hair.

Man 1: Who's he?

Man 2: Ding Jianguo.

Man 1: Who's Ding Jianguo?

Woman 1: Wang Guoqing's hand is shaking.

Man 1: How come this gun's so heavy? My face's hot. It's tears. How come I'm crying? I'm crying in front of him?

(*Wang Guoqing looks at Ding Jianguo. He slowly lowers the gun. Ding looks at him in shock.*)

Man 1: Rain drips from the tip of his nose, a long drip. Why's he crying?

Man 2: (*extends his hand*) I shouldn't have let you carry the sin of murder. I should've carried it.

Woman 1: Wang Guoqing looks at Ding Jianguo. The hand he extends is shaking.

Man 2: I know that gun is loaded. Actually, no big deal.

(*Wang hands the gun back slowly.*)

Woman 1: Suddenly, Wang Guoqing lifts his arm

and flings the gun away. It falls into the sea, without a trace.

(*Wang throws the gun away.*)

Man 3: Silence.

Woman 1: Wind, blowing more fiercely.

Man 3: Silence.

Woman 2: Rain, falling harder.

Man 3: Silence.

Woman 3: The sea crashes at the embankment.

Man 3: Hong Kong, Central, by the sea. In the rain. Wang Guoqing, Ding Jianguo. They stand face to face silently.

(*Wang Guoqing turns around to leave. He walks away rapidly. Man 3, Woman 1, Woman 2 and Woman 3 follow him.*)

(*Ding Jianguo slumps on the floor. The light on him dims.*)

Woman 2: There's not a soul on the streets.

Woman 3: A hint of murky white creeps in the edge of the sky.

Woman 1: The city's becoming clearer gradually.

Woman 2: Rain. When did it stop?

Woman 3: Wind. When did it stop?

Woman 1: Wang Guoqing walks rapidly.

Man 1: I look up. The cloud's gone. Only the empty sky. Pale and pallid.

Man 3: Wang Guoqing falls over suddenly.

(*Wang Guoqing falls over suddenly.*)

Woman 1: A crow. That crow.

Woman 2: A crow on the ground.

Woman 3: A dead crow on the ground.

Man 3: It lays there stiffly.

Woman 1: A street cleaner heads over.

Woman 2: Hi, you all right?

Man 1: Yeah.

Woman 1: She sweeps the crow into the pan.

Man 1: I'm being swept into the pan by that woman, then tipped into the bin. My stiff body hits the bin with a thud.

Woman 1: Look, how sad.

Man 1: Yeah, really sad.

Woman 2: Wang Guoqing climbs up.

(*Wang Guoqing climbs up.*)

Man 1: Eh? Where's the crowd?

Woman 2: Gone.

Man 1: That many people, gone?

Woman 1: Yeah, gone. Life's hard enough. Don't go starting things blindly, ah!

Woman 3: The cleaner goes away.

Woman 1: The streets are deserted.

(*Woman Standing on the street, Wang Guoqing feels the cold.*)

Man 1: So cold.

Woman 2: Where do you think you're going?

Man 1: Who?

Woman 3: You.

Man 1: Me?

Woman 1: Yes, you. Wang Guoqing.

Woman 2: Silence.

Man 1: I don't know.

Woman 3: Silence.

Man 3: Wang Guoqing seems to have heard a gunshot.

Man 1: I seem to have heard a gunshot.

(*A loud gunshot*)

(*Blackout*)

Character: Man 1
                Man 2
                Man 3
                Woman 1
                Woman 2
                Woman 3
Location: Theatre
Time: Now

(*Lights up*)

(*People stand in the middle of the stage, dressed all in black.*)

    Man 3: (*exaggerated*) A murder of crow. They're thirsty, looking for water everywhere.

    Man 2: The crows see a bottle. Water inside.

    Man 1: But not much. The bottle's neck's small. The crows can't get to it. What to do?

    Woman 1: What to do?

    Woman 2: What to do?

    Woman 3: What to do?

    Man 1: The crows die from thirst.

    Man 2: We die from thirst, on the pebbles.

Man 3: If I'm alone, that'd be great. (*Looks at his watch*) Nine thirty in the evening. Theatre. Curtains. Performance over. Audience leaves.

(*Light dims.*)

2015 香港藝術節新劇本選——烏合之眾
HKAF New Play Selection 2015——The Crowd

督 印 人 Publisher	何 嘉 坤 Tisa Ho
主 編 Editor	余 瑞 婷 Susanna Yu
平 面 設 計 Graphic Design	Kenneth Lo
出 版 Publisher	香 港 藝 術 節 協 會 有 限 公 司 Hong Kong Arts Festival Society Ltd.
出 版 顧 問 Publishing Consultant	MCCM Creations
版 次 Edition	2015 年 3 月 初 版 1st edition, March 2015
書 號 ISBN	978-988-16056-8-9
定 價 Price	港 幣 HK$120

烏合之眾劇本版權 © 2015 喻榮軍
© 2015 The Crowd script, Yu Rongjun

版權垂詢 Copyright Enquiry：

香港藝術節協會有限公司
Hong Kong Arts Festival Society Ltd.
香港灣仔港灣道二號十二字樓1205室
12/F, 2/F Harbour Road, Wan Chai, Hong Kong.
電話 Tel：(852) 2824 3555
傳真 Fax：(852) 2824 3798 / 2824 3722
電郵 Email：afgen@hkaf.org
網頁 Website：www.hk.artsfestival.org

版權所有 翻印必究 All rights reserved.